What People Are Saying About
Learning to Balance Your Life . . .

"Since I first met her twenty years ago, Sharon's life and work served as a lighthouse beacon to lost and wandering souls like me and millions of others. That she would continue to be so, to continue to call us toward a path she has personally traveled with such style and grace through this stage of life should come as no surprise. Well done again, Sharon."

Ted Klontz
CEO Onsite Workshops,
Nashville, TN

"Sharon Wegscheider-Cruse offers a book filled with time-honored truths spoken in the language of today. This one book can make a big difference in your life. It's filled with the kind of spiritual and practical wisdom that can bring peace to your inner and outer worlds. It lights a path. Take the actions that will bring your life and your spirit into harmony so that you can get the most out of the life you already have."

Tian Dayton
author, therapist

"Sharon has consistently been an explorer of life, meaning and purpose. Her work, observation and guidance toward 'balance' in one's life are based on her great love of life and experience. I am glad she has decided to share an organized approach to "balance" in one's life."

Bill O'Donnell
founder, Miraval Life in Balance Spa

Author of the Bestseller *Learning to Love Yourself*
Sharon Wegscheider-Cruse

Learning to Balance Your Life

6 Powers that Restore Your Energy and Spirit

With a Foreword by Mark Bryan
Cofounder of *The Artist's Way*, Author, *The Artist's Way at Work*

Health Communications, Inc.
Deerfield Beach, Florida

www.bcibooks.com

**Library of Congress Cataloging-in-Publication Data
is available at the Library of Congress**

2005190210

Publisher: Health Communications, Inc.
            3201 S.W. 15th Street
            Deerfield Beach, FL 33442-8190

Cover design by Larissa Hise Henoch
Inside book design by Dawn Von Strolley Grove

This book is dedicated to my children,
Pat, Sandra and Deborah;
their partners, Phil, Tom and Andy;
my grandchildren, Matthew, Melanie,
Christopher, Ryan, Cheyenne, Sierra and Andy Jr.;
my sister, Sue, and most especially,
my soul mate, Joe Cruse.
This group of people makes my world go 'round.

CONTENTS

FOREWORD

*F*ew authors in the self-help section of your bookstore can honestly claim—though many falsely do—to have started a true social movement. Rarer still is the person whose teachings have actually helped (not just claimed to help) millions of people, providing encouragement, insight and legitimate guidance for their lives. Sharon Wegscheider-Cruse is one of these precious few.

Sharon's first book, *Another Chance: Hope and Health for the Alcoholic Family,* changed the language of addiction recovery to include the family and became a mainstay for self-help and recovery programs around the world. The book won the Marty Mann Award for outstanding contribution on alcoholism as a family disease and helped found the fellowship of ACoA (Adult Children of Alcoholics). Both the book and her workshops are widely used in the treatment of substance abuse and are part of many collegiate and medical school curriculums.

In the early 1980s, while reading everything I could find about human interactions and how families become successful (or don't), I came across Sharon's work. A friend in Chicago recommended it to me, saying Sharon's ideas had changed his life—no small claim. Curious, I went out and bought *Another Chance* and read it straight through.

That book changed the way I made sense of the world: Sharon's descriptions of the family as a system of interlocking roles—the hero, the scapegoat, the mascot and the lost child—became my layman's introduction to what would later become my scientific passion: the study of systems theory and how people act in groups. I am still grateful for that initial inspiration.

People seek counseling from all sorts of places—clergy, therapists, support groups and self-help books. We seek guidance for all kinds of problems—addictions, marital strife, heartbreak, career setbacks or even how to get teenagers to do their homework. Human beings are curious animals. We are programmed to seek knowledge. This trait is what makes us human—we have ambition and a drive to know the truth.

Unfortunately, when we enter counseling or read our first self-help book, we are usually focused on getting out of the pain we are in at the moment. We focus on the past, the pain or the problem and rarely on our power, our strengths or our gratitude. Of course, looking at the past for clues to our present is part of standard psychological detective work—it is necessary and important. But what do we do once we are on our feet again? How do we learn to focus on our power and not our past? This question is the essential thrust of Sharon's new work.

Learning to Balance Your Life focuses on the human success factors—our innate powers to communicate, collaborate and cope—and provides a plan for achieving success in every area of our lives.

Sharon's previous work became a movement that helped raise our sights from the individual to the system at large. Her new movement introduces us to power—what it is and how to attain it—and asks us to stop viewing life through our histories and to start looking at the future through our strengths. It is a profound shift of focus.

Power, classically defined, is "the ability to do or act," a "particular faculty of mind or body," or more colloquially, the ability to get things done. The word itself has gotten a bad rap lately as people confuse it with a philosophy of greed or as a rationale for unethical behavior. If we are honest with ourselves, many of us think of power in terms of purchasing power or power at our jobs—and we will increase them if we can. This is a fact of human nature. But how happy or secure are we when money or status begins to matter above all else?

Thankfully the powers described here owe more to the world's wisdom traditions than to Machiavellian maneuvering. Recent research on group dynamics validates this approach. The fact is, humans have gotten just as far, if not farther, from cooperation than from competition. (Not that competing is a bad thing—it is an important aspect of life). But morality is important: true and lasting power comes from forthrightness and connection, not deception or cutthroat competition.

This book details the critical powers of the human experience. Sharon describes them as mental power, emotional power, spiritual power, physical power, social power and our will power. Balanced together, they result in our being as powerful as we are meant to be. The book offers exercises to help us understand, measure and increase the individual powers. Taken together, they energize each other and become our tickets to achievement no matter what our histories, educations or financial statuses. Enjoy the added voltage—it might just light the world.

Mark Bryan
cofounder, The Artist's Way
author, *The Artist's Way at Work*,
The Prodigal Father and *Money Drunk, Money Sober*

ACKNOWLEDGMENTS

I am indebted to the following people for helping me bring this book to fruition. Having partners not only brings valuable contributions to the work, but also makes writing so much more interesting and fun.

My first thank-you goes to my editor, Patrick Cotter, who became a true partner in putting this book together. His insight and skill is evident in the book's readability. He enlightened, challenged and assisted me in making sure this text says what I wanted it to say. When he commented, "The essence of writing is re-writing," it gave me that extra bit of freedom to create—and recreate—as I went. Thanks, Pat. I would work with you anytime.

My second thank-you goes to my soul mate, Joseph Cruse. He listened for hours as I worked out what I wanted to say—distilling some former work, adding new ideas and concepts, yet wanting to keep the book simple, straightforward and, above all, useful. He continues to be my sounding board and jumps right in with help when I ask for it. I can't imagine writing a book without your feedback, Joe.

My third thank-you goes to Richard Dorchak, Sr., who did the illustrations for the book. Oftentimes a sketch provides the clarity that is needed for understanding a concept. Working with you, Richard, in visualizing several important parts of the book, felt like being a kid with a new box of crayons again. That was fun.

I also want to thank Gary Seidler, Peter Vegso, Pat Holdsworth, Allison Janse and Penelope Love, as well as the HCI editorial, production and marketing and sales teams for their efforts in bringing this book to the world.

PREFACE

I love telling stories that help people change their lives and make this world a better place to live. I've been telling stories since 1981, when my first book, *Another Chance: Hope and Health for the Alcoholic Family*, became a bestseller. Since then, I have published several other books and produced two successful educational films. It is very gratifying to know that my stories—many of them translated into other languages—have helped change lives around the world. My own life changed when I retired a few years ago from a very active and fulfilling career. I soon found that retirement to me meant *redirection*—and that has helped bring about this new story. There has been so much new learning and so many new experiences in that redirection. A trip around the world taught me brand new lessons about the way I want to live. And I read a wonderful book by Julia Cameron that reawakened my creative juices. The book, *The Artist's Way*, challenged me to keep active and contributing. As Bernard Baruch said, "A man can't retire his experience. He must use it. Experience achieves more with less energy and time."

Cameron's book also reminded me that we couldn't teach what we have not experienced. So I set out to experience my life again with focus and not just drift through it. Cameron's words made me pay attention to all of who I am. I have always believed in wholeness, so I set out to expand my whole range of experience and my sense of all the possibilities open to me—my wholeness. I liked what I found in my travels:

- The grandeur of ancient ruins in Mexico and Rome, the fantastic spectacle of nature's power in the lava spills in Hawaii and the total isolation of Easter Island
- The universal energy that radiates in holy shrines of India, the vortex of Sedona, on the path of the Lakota Sioux at Bear Butte in South Dakota and in the footsteps of St. Paul and the Blessed Virgin Mary in Ephesus, Turkey
- The wisdom and tranquility that come from sitting at the feet of spiritual masters and meditating in spiritual centers around the world
- The power of the battleground at Normandy Beach and what the courage of the men who fought and died there meant to the safety of the United States and to peace in the world

I treasure each experience because it reinforces my awareness that *spirit* is everywhere. However, the most exciting and comforting place to be is within me, when I spend the time and energy to go within and explore the gifts I have been given. They, in turn, have given me a place in the world and direction on how to live, make decisions and serve the people in my life.

The spiritual challenges are there, and the spiritual directions are there. In rising to the challenges, accepting direction and taking the actions that are assigned to me, I find satisfaction and fulfillment. This brings me happiness. This process is there for all of us, and all of us can find increased satisfaction, fulfillment and happiness.

These beliefs and my experiences gave me the focus for writing this book. The changing story of my own life has shown me the need for finding balance in life in order to become the people we want to be with the energy and connection to spirit that are at the heart of a full life.

The information I present about balancing your life is not difficult to understand; the challenge is making the decisions and following through on them to actualize your own life. It is essential to balance your life in order to find fulfillment, satisfaction and meaning. When people are in partnership or families, and each lives a life in balance, relationships become stronger and more meaningful. We all can make our corner of the world a better place to live. I invite you to listen to my newest story, which is about increasing your energy and awakening your spirit to create a balanced life. As the Buddhist saying goes:

When the student is ready,
the teacher will appear.

How to Use This Book: Action Tools

Each chapter on your six personal powers (chapters two through seven) will provide you with a deeper understanding of the power's meaning and importance in your life, as well as encourage you to reawaken that power's potential for change and personal fulfillment. A better understanding of your six personal powers will give you new insights, energy and direction in all areas of your life, but you must put this information to work. In other words, you must *act!* Information without action leads to frustration and depression. Informed action enlivens the spirit and encourages transformation.

To help you take healthy actions, each chapter contains three reader tools that encourage you to examine your life, pinpoint the areas you would like to change, design an action plan to make those changes and monitor your progress along the way.

Near the beginning of each power chapter, you will find a self-assessment checklist called "Signs of a Power Outage." When we chronically neglect one or more of our personal powers, we often experience a lack of energy and clarity—and a great deal of indecision. I call this state a "time of power outage." The self-assessment checklist will help you gauge any personal "power outages" you may be experiencing and encourage you to start repairing them.

> *The value of an idea lies in the using of it.*
> —*Thomas Alva Edison*

At the end of each personal power chapter you will find two potent tools for assessing your current life situation in depth and designing action plans that will change your life.

The "Power Generators" worksheet is your personalized homework assignment and asks you to engage in specific "power" activities designed to stretch your potential power and enrich your life.

The "Power Journal" worksheets that follow invite you to design a blueprint for active change and to commit to your action plans for at least eight weeks. I suggest you set aside a weekly block of time (I call mine "the weekly check-in") to evaluate how you are doing and to make any needed adjustments to your blueprint. You can do this alone, by turning your worksheets into an ongoing journal. You can also work with a group of friends on a weekly basis, sharing details of your action plan and any progress you have made. In some situations, you may want to work with a coach or therapist to help you through the process.

Once you choose a way to awaken your spirit by developing your six personal powers, stick with it for at least eight weeks. Be faithful, and watch for any changes that begin to happen. If you like what is happening, commit to as many additional eight-week sessions as you choose.

1

THE POWER OF BALANCE

The best and safest thing is to keep a balance in your life, acknowledge the great powers around us and in us. If you can do that and live that way, you really are wise.

Euripides

I'm Entitled to Have It All (and So Are You)

Like most people, I want to have it all. Why shouldn't I? Life is a wonderful and exciting journey. I am an ordinary person getting to live an extraordinary life. My life has been blessed with many wondrous relationships. I count among my friends some millionaires and a couple of billionaires. I know many retired couples living on tight budgets and young parents working hard to raise children. Included in my inner circle are gay friends, single friends, creative artists and business giants. My blessings include healers, inventors, musicians and what my grandmother used to refer to as "good" people. By that, she meant people who were *spirited* and full of caring energy.

I still love to ride the merry-go-round at Disney World, sing "Amazing Grace" in any church and go to temple with friends. I have watched the births of my children and my grandchildren. I have come to know the joy of them throwing their arms around me and telling me they love me. The intimacy I feel with my soul mate as we cuddle down in bed warms my heart, my body and my soul.

Sometimes I feel like I am in sync with it all, but at other times, I feel empty and overwhelmed. When I put too many appointments and obligations on my calendar, I start to feel overwhelmed. When it's easier to say "yes," rather than disappoint someone, or when I procrastinate and everything starts to happen at once, I feel tense. By the time I fulfill all my commitments, I feel empty and without energy. I know enough not to get into these kinds of binds, but occasionally I just slip and do it anyway.

Sometimes relationships work, but at other times they bring me sadness and pain. My relationships work when I pay attention to them and do my part. All relationships need the sharing of time and energy. I need to invest and be fully present to the person I am in relationship with. When I am over busy or scattered, it's hard to feel close to me or anyone else.

There is a lot going on all the time. There are periods when everything is going well in one part of my life and things in other parts of my life aren't going so well. Does it have to be like this? Is there a way to have it all and—at the same time—a life in balance?

I have found that if we go after what we want with intensity, we get most of what we want. It is when we try to have it all without maintaining balance that there is a very good chance there will be negative consequences. Some part—or parts—of our lives will be less than satisfying. I think the following quote from Bryan Dyson, who served as CEO of Coca-Cola for twenty-five years, concisely sums up just how crucial balance is to our lives:

Imagine life as a game in which you are juggling five balls in the air. You name them—work, family, health, friends and spirit—and you're keeping all of these in the air. You will soon understand that work is a rubber ball. If you drop it, it will bounce back. But the other four balls—family, health, friends and spirit—are made of glass. If you drop one of these, they will be irrevocably scuffed, marked, nicked, damaged or even shattered. They will never be the same. You must understand that and strive for balance in your life.

Life Out of Balance:
The Too-Many Syndrome

We see the consequences of lack of balance all around us. I call it the "too-many syndrome."

- Too many restaurants, too much of the wrong foods and too little exercise results in too many pounds.
- Too many commitments and too much saying "yes" result in resentment and fatigue.
- Too many toxic and superficial relationships and too much wasted time in meaningless relationships result in loneliness and boredom.
- Too much focus on superficial concerns instead of spiritual concerns, too little caring for others and too many actions based on trivial needs instead of compassionate values result in emptiness and restlessness.
- Too much alcohol, too much nicotine and too much medication (whether legal or illegal drugs) result in blocked feelings, emotional unavailability and diminished sexual ability.
- Too much work, too many hours at work and too much preoccupation with work result in lack of intimacy, lack of time to play and diminished sexual ability.

At the same time, there is a superabundance of solutions to having too much, too many, too often. For years, we have been glutted with books on diet, healthful eating and recipes. Yet we remain a nation of people of all ages struggling with weight issues and obesity. We have parks, gyms and exercise equipment available to us, and yet we are a sedentary people. We have churches, synagogues, countless ways to worship, a steady stream of books and workshops, and yet people are starving for a way to find and express their spirituality. We have a technology designed to make our lives simpler and easier. Yet computers, e-mail and cell phones tend to add a level of stress, rather than help us find ways to live with less stress.

> *Just as your car runs more smoothly and requires less energy to go faster and farther when the wheels are in perfect alignment, you perform better when your thoughts, feelings, emotions, goals and values are in balance.*
> —Brian Tracy

Perhaps we have never lived in a time with so many choices, but paradoxically, many feel that there are so few choices. To them, things seem to be wrong, to be out of balance.

Restoring Balance

In some ways, the very excess of solutions sometimes is part of the problem. Whole sections of bookstores offer guides and programs that suggest six of this, seven of that and maybe four of something else to ensure some specific outcome, whether financial success, rewarding

> *It takes as much energy to wish as it does to plan.*
> —Eleanor Roosevelt

relationships, good health, spirituality, recovery from addiction, etc.

These books may contain helpful points, but our lives are not so simple. Six steps to success for us might not work if someone we love is depressed. Seven steps to spirituality might not work if we are fifty pounds overweight. Four plans for happiness might not be enough if our love relationship is sour.

Too often, these guides and programs focus on behaviors and outcomes. They promise that the reader will become a whole person by following certain steps to achieve certain goals. While they may often achieve these goals, people still feel unfulfilled, incomplete and restless because there is always another goal to achieve in another area. Many self-help solutions try to change the person's inside by changing the person's outside: the job, the partner, the body image, the bank account, the spiritual awareness, etc. They don't focus on the *whole* person.

> *Dream no small dreams*
> *for they have no power*
> *to move the hearts of*
> *men.*
>
> —Goethe

My personal and professional experience has convinced me that the transformation to wholeness comes from the inside out. In order to feel whole, when every area of our life is in balance, we have to have full access to what I call our *personal power.* It seems to me that wholeness, personal power and health are our natural way of being. Wholeness is what happens when we make decisions to live in balance rather than out of balance. First we value and heal ourselves, then our relationships. We then take this way of living into the world.

We need to use all of our personal power to *live all*

parts of our life at the same time. It doesn't work to have just spirituality one day, lovers the next day and exercise on the third day. We need to use all parts of ourselves in all areas of our lives in all the days we are given.

It may sound overwhelming, but it isn't. We just need to be willing to look at our twenty-four-hour gift of time and pay attention to our resources and our expenditure of energy—our powers. It's like money. There is just so much we have and so much we can afford to spend each day. Our energy and power resources need equally careful handling.

> *Thoughts create a new heaven, a new firmament, a new source of energy, from which new arts flow.*
>
> —Paracelsus

With the body we received at birth, each of us also received an energy resource, which is often called our *spirit* or our *power*. We sometimes hear people say, "She sure has a lot of spirit," or "He's a powerful person." What they're really saying is that there is an indefinable quality about such people that separates them from others. An energy power spirit enables them to stand out in a crowd.

That energy comes from how well that person has developed the power that came with his or her body. When there has been a healthy and balanced development of personal power, energy and spirit are released. When there is a blockage of personal power, there are consequences that diminish our capacity for life. There is a lack of spirit.

> *Healing does not mean becoming physically well—it means finding a balance between physical, intellectual, spiritual and emotional dimensions.*
>
> —Elizabeth Kübler-Ross

Learning to Balance Your Life describes the personal

powers or energies that we all have, the blockages that keep people from tapping into their power, the consequences of these blockages and how to recapture personal power to increase energy and awaken the spirit.

It's simple to read about all of this and easy to understand what happens, what is needed and what one can expect. It's *hard* to make the commitment to change one's life, act and start making those changes on a daily basis.

Energy and persistence alter all things.
—Benjamin Franklin

While *Learning to Balance Your Life* offers helpful information and guidance, my goal in writing this book is to help awaken—or reawaken—the spirit or energy inside you that lets you live your life to the fullest. Consider it an invitation to a journey of transformation. *Learning to Balance Your Life* offers a new understanding of what our possibilities and potential are all about—and details the spiritual and emotional transformation required to realize them. It is about making the commitment to change one decisive day at a time. In doing so, you can create balance in your life. You will be able to see your life *start* to change in just eight weeks. The change may be dramatic or subtle. However, as you increase the balance in your life, the rewards will be yours for years to come.

Our Six Personal Powers

Each of us has six personal powers that we are born with. And each of us has twenty-four hours a day to develop, apply or ignore our power sources. These powers have potential, just as electricity does. Each power's potential acts and interacts with each of the other powers. This interaction is called *wholeness*. Think of wholeness as an electrical circuit that enables electricity to flow any-where and everywhere you want it to.

Spiritual energy flows in and produces effects in the phenomenal world.
—William James

Each power also has its own importance. Each can exist in balance and therefore in harmony with the others, but not at their expense. Rather, each gives richness to the other powers. When we become whole and all our powers are functioning, we can work toward achieving health, happiness, security and satisfaction in relation-ships—whatever we desire.

- **Will Power** is the ability to make choices, to change directions when desired and to follow through with decisions.
- **Spiritual Power** is the ability to believe in some-thing outside yourself, to define and live according to your values and to feel connectedness.
- **Emotional Power** is the ability to feel all your feel-ings, express them appropriately and prevent feel-ings from becoming blocked.
- **Social Power** is the ability to love and be loved and to have satisfying relationships with family and friends.
- **Physical Power** is the ability to care for your body (through nutrition, rest, dress), to exercise and use your body, and to be sensual and sexual.
- **Mental Power** is the ability to remember the past and use it, to be functional and perform in the pre-sent, and to imagine, dream and plan for the future.

The Power Wheel

Well-wrought, balanced wheels roll with great efficiency, enabling a minimum application of power for maximum movement. Our six personal powers also comprise a sort of power wheel, working in concert to provide the unbroken flow of energy we need to live fully.

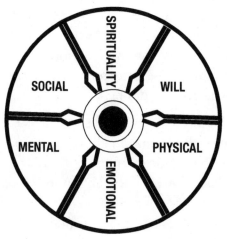

Now picture one part of the wheel as broken or flat. This affects the wheel as a whole, and it will not roll with the same efficiency or function—just like a flat tire. If more than one part of the wheel is broken, the wheel simply won't work.

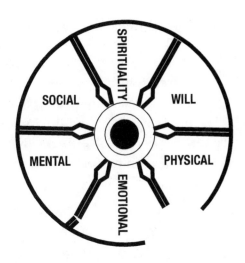

Our personal powers function like that wheel. If any one of our powers is neglected, the whole is affected, and we are basically riding through life on a flat tire. While all the powers are essential, our spiritual power connects us to a power greater than ourselves and opens up the greatest potential in life. So it is the first among equals.

Power-Less and Power-Full People

Our bodies need energy to operate efficiently in all areas of life. At different times we run on high, low, empty or somewhere in between. We require continuous recharging and unblocked energy flow to have the power to live fully in every area of life simultaneously.

There are, however, people who struggle with the concept of identifying with personal powers. These people experience a sort of permanent power outage at

> *Power can be taken, but not given. The process of the taking is empowerment in itself.*
>
> —*Gloria Steinem*

some level. They never really connect with their own spirit and so lack the energy to engage life to the fullest. Power outages can occur in any and every dimension of our lives—spiritual, emotional, social, physical, mental and in the exercise of our wills. We all know people who have power outages in one or more of the six personal powers:

- Jean has a serious will outage. She is talented, fun, smart and attractive. Yet in both her career and her primary relationship, she just can't say "no." She takes on more than anyone can possibly do. Jean comes from a family of means, and she feels bad for anyone who does not have the privileges that she has enjoyed. She spends a great deal of time volunteering and often wears herself out trying to do too much. Her sister Cindy has a similar problem with her family. She is the one who is always there taking care of her parents. She even gave up a chance for marriage because she didn't want to move to another state where her fiancé was being transferred. She just couldn't say "no" when her mother asked her to stay behind and be there for her. Both sisters suffer from an inability to say "no."

- Janet experiences a spiritual outage. She is a totally pragmatic person who cannot accept any of the spiritual aspects of life. Janet truly believes that everything is logical and practical and that there are reasons for everything. It is hard for her to imagine anything outside of herself affecting her life. She feels totally responsible for herself and totally in control.

- Kevin suffers from an emotional outage. He resists feelings by not sharing his emotions with other people. He believes his feelings are his private business and, he says, he doesn't have many feelings to begin with. Kevin medicates himself with both nicotine and alcohol. He smokes a pack of cigarettes a day and occasionally has quite a bit to drink. Other ways people can self-medicate is with workaholism, sexual acting out, drugs, gambling, etc. The more someone self-medicates, the more his or her true feelings become buried—like Kevin's. This denial of an emotional life can lead to depression.

- Barbara has a social outage. She still experiences pain about things that happened growing up in her family. The past hurt and abandonment that she experienced with her family carried into her marriage. When that marriage ended, she felt as though all her relationships were going to be painful, and she now shies away from all close attachments. Barbara feels a great deal of loneliness and emptiness. She keeps her relationships with coworkers and friends at a superficial level because of her fear of abandonment.

- Tom struggles with mental and physical outages. While he is a brilliant man and a computer expert, he is so wrapped up in his work that other parts of his life suffer. He can spend hours focused on the computer screen and loves all the possibilities the computer offers him. He tends to neglect his physical health and is both overweight and sedentary. His doctor has told him that he needs to exercise and lose weight, but Tom just doesn't take the time to follow his doctor's orders. Since his weight gain, Tom has felt less attractive and less sexual.

These power-less people fall into two groups—the resisters and the avoiders. Both lack the energy to change their lives. Resistance and avoidance happen to most people to a certain degree some of the time. It's human nature. This becomes a problem when it becomes a way of life that prevents us from using our powers to impact life situations.

There are also people who understand and accept the potential, as well as the risks, of opening up to the power within them and the people and places around them. I call these people the embracers because they embrace life's full potential. Embracers face the temptation to resist and to avoid from time to time. But they choose to jump into life, face what needs to be faced and make decisions that give them the most flexibility and power, and the biggest personal payoff. They make their own luck.

Let's take a closer look at each group.

Resisters

To this group, looking at oneself and thinking about possibilities and change is a scary prospect. These people are resistant to change and avoid any possibility of vulnerability at all costs. They mask their fear by calling it boredom. The prospect for profound change is not for them; they see it as too simplistic or irrelevant. These people literally resist the flow of energy for change and remain insulated from life. They miss so much in life because they think they already know everything—at least in the limited world they have created for themselves. They have already defined what they believe success, spirituality, values and fun to be, and they stop searching, learning and exploring the world. Denial is part of the process. Resisters often do not recognize their resistance. They feel they know all they need to know. This arrogance leads to restlessness in the soul that needs calming. There are many ways to quiet the inner turmoil: busyness, projects, sex, money, alcohol, drugs, shopping, etc.

Avoiders

Avoiders have lots of plans and ideas. But the morning paper comes and they get a slow start. Then they need to answer their e-mail and phone messages. They allow any outside distraction to stop them from focusing on their lives. They keep unplugging themselves from the flow of energy, and so they never generate a sustained forward movement. This is a sure way to have little or no balance in life, and these people rarely have enough time for anything they want to accomplish. Actually, they never really get started. Perfectionism is a big part of the avoider. If you don't get started, you can't fail.

Whether people are avoiders or resisters, the result is the same. They continue to feel restless, bored and empty, and they don't know why.

Embracers

Embracers are power-full people, or people with the capacity to become power-full. They sincerely want to grow personally and connect with others to find meaning, satisfaction and happiness in life. They aren't sure where their paths are going to take them, but they are willing to:

- Learn or try new behaviors and experience a bigger range of feelings.
- Reexamine their lives, leave behind toxic people, behaviors, habits and attitudes, and reinvent themselves with new interests and hobbies.
- Leave some things to the universe and have trust when they make decisions and choices.
- Look for the spirit in their lives and seek their own personal truth.

Waking up to Life's Richness

Spiritual transformation and power generation take place when knowledge and experience meet, just as electricity flows from the interplay of positive and negative charges.

In the world to come, each of us will be called to account for all the good things God put on earth that we refused to enjoy.

—*Talmud*

When we've learned enough and hurt enough to know that we can't go back to the way our lives used to be—but we don't know how to go forward yet—we can choose to *stop*. In that stopping, we find our inner wisdom and listen to our own spiritual power. We can then make the choices and changes that will alter our lives. This process is called transformation.

Stopping whatever we are doing doesn't mean inaction and passivity. It means giving up control and using our inner resources to decide how we want to live. The first step is facing our own avoidance, resistance, denial and minimizing, and then asking for help to admit to and confront our compulsions and self-defeating behaviors. Getting more information just won't do it. Having additional information without acting and making changes leads to frustration and depression. The chapter on will power offers suggestions for making choices, taking actions and creating change.

The second transformative step is to wake up emotionally. We have to let our feelings surface and explore all the ways we might run away from our feelings. We talk about our feelings and use them to understand others and ourselves. The chapter on emotional power addresses how to do this.

The third step is to accept and forgive. We accept reality and truth. We see ourselves in relationship to others. We are aware of everyone and everything around us. We take responsibility for ourselves and forgive when it is important to do so. The chapter on social power helps us look at the relationships where we need to practice acceptance and forgiveness.

Next we take the step to enlightenment. This means recognizing a power outside of ourselves as the truth and learning when the spirit is working within us. We usually only know of spirit's presence after the fact. It leaves us feeling warmth, love, hope, understanding and a sense of well-being. The absence of spirit leaves us feeling alone, discouraged, disillusioned, separate and in pain.

The last step of transformation is to know and experience closeness and connectedness in our relationships. We know at our core that we matter to some person or to many people—a partner, a child, a sibling, family, friends or a community. The intimacy we all crave in life comes to us when we know how to be a "spirit person."

When we undergo a spiritual transformation, we experience the world in a different way. We see reality for what it is and understand that it is up to us to change and to move closer to a higher power that will sustain our energy and adjust our lives so we stay connected as spirit people.

Spirit People

Becoming a spirit person is not for the fainthearted or half-hearted. It's not an easy transformation. It's only for those who are willing to do what it takes to reclaim their own spirit and soul. How do you recognize spirit people?

1. Spirit people resist conformity. They know they have a gift. It may be writing, organizing, speaking, sports, music, medicine, homemaking, art, business, etc. There are countless gifts, and spirit people are willing to use and develop their gifts, no matter what.

2. Spirit people know how to say "no" as well as "yes." They do not waste time on nonessentials. They listen to their inner self and follow their own intuition. They are focused and do not have time to dawdle.

3. Spirit people give up their need to understand and

control people and events.

4. Spirit people know they need to protect themselves from information overload and too many stimulating experiences. They know the dangers of drowning in information but starving for wisdom. Someone once gave me a banner that said, "It's good to be a seeker and a learner, but sooner or later it's time to take what we have learned and begin to share it with anybody who will listen."

> *God will send His angels to take good care of you. After all, it is those who have a deep and real inner life who are able to deal with the irritating details of our outer life.*
>
> —Evelyn Underhill

5. Spirit people are also aware of—and accept—life's miracles. Webster's defines a miracle as "an event that appears unexplainable by laws of nature and so is held to be an act of God." Spiritual power not only enables miracles, but also enables us to understand when they occur.

When I was a little girl, I grew up in poverty, and alcoholism was a big part of my family history. Formal education was limited and so were possibilities for the future. How, then, did I grow up to be a woman who is educated and considered successful?

I celebrate three wonderful adult children, their three special partners and seven grandchildren. My life is spent with a loving soul mate and countless loving family and friends. My work has great meaning and satisfaction for me. One day I said to myself, "It must be a miracle, this life of mine." There was no other way to understand it. It's the only explanation. As I search and explore my life,

I discover many miracles. Chances are, there are miracles in your life as well. This book will show you how to see them more clearly and to make more miracles happen.

2

WILL POWER

What we do today, at this very moment, will have a cumulative effect on all our tomorrows.

Alexandra Stoddard

Power to Choose

Will power is the ability and willingness to make choices. It's consciously directing energy to support the choices we make. When we make good choices for ourselves, it's our ticket to freedom and possibility. We can make the kind of lives we want for ourselves. We can take our experience, our values, our relationships, our beliefs and our bodies and make choices that tie all our life together and move us in the direction of our dreams.

We can set goals, establish priorities and persevere until we achieve our goals. I am not talking about will power as traditionally understood, the moralistic "should" concerning some ideal behavior or the need to sacrifice to meet someone else's standard. I am not

---

Will Power: Signs of a Power Outage

(check any that apply)

___ I often feel overwhelmed.

___ I often feel too busy.

___ I am consistently late.

___ I often conform to others' needs and wishes.

___ I have a hard time saying "no."

___ I often procrastinate.

___ I avoid asking for what I want and need.

___ I frequently avoid making decisions.

___ I avoid risky decisions.

___ I often feel resentful and victimized.

___ I am often indecisive.

referring to the power to conform to rigid rules that many grew up with. I am talking about having a *will strong enough to make decisions that are in our best interests.* This is *will power* in the best sense of the term. Doing what others expect of us certainly limits our possibilities. Making choices that are dictated by old standards or another's expectations or wishes is not going to be very satisfying.

> *When I was a kid, they told me to do what my parents wanted. When I became an adult, they told me to do what my kids wanted. When do I get what I want?*
>
> —*Sam Levenson*

Doing Our Best

We can all do the best we can each day. Let's look at that twenty-four hours we have every day. If we try to do more than is possible in that allotted time, we are going to feel tired and depleted. If we choose not to use our twenty-four hours in a positive way, we will feel frustrated and restless.

> *In the end, it's not the years in your life that count, it's the life in your years.*
>
> —*Abraham Lincoln*

We can choose to do our best whether we are working, resting or playing. That's our choice. As we do our best in every area of our lives, our best keeps improving. We must play as well as work. We must exercise as well as rest. We must address each of the areas of our lives each day. We are not here to sacrifice joy. We are here to be happy and to love.

When we get so busy and caught up in the details of daily living, we miss out on the big things in life. We have the capacity to choose whether our destinies— "the seemingly inevitable succession of events"—will be something we suffer or something we celebrate.

Choose to Make It Happen: Start Now

Being happy and fulfilled is about action. *It is not only about knowing.* All the knowing in the world cannot guarantee happiness. We need to be active. Everyone wants to be thin and healthy, so we have a huge industry producing diet books, diet plans, and diet and exercise magazines. Yet we have a record number of people who are inactive, overweight and obese. We want the information, but we don't want to take the time or make the commitment to change our lifestyles or our eating habits.

Use your mortality to get the most out of life. Saying "no" to someone else is like saying "yes" to yourself.

—Bernie Siegel

We are all artists and decision makers when it comes to designing our own lives. Talking and philosophizing are easy. Taking action and changing our lives are risky and hard, but worth it. In other words—as I'm fond of saying— instead of waiting for someone to send you flowers, plant a garden!

To live a creative life, we must lose our fear of being wrong.

—Joseph Chilton Pearce

No Wasted Decisions

We are often held back from a decision because we are afraid of making the wrong decision. It would be better to look at decisions as opportunities. If we make a decision and are happy with the way it turns out, good for us. It was the right decision. If we don't like the way it turns out, we can use it as a learning experience and not repeat that decision. People who make choices are willing to take risks. They know that there is no reward without risk.

Choice makers always come out ahead. Either way they get something from the decision. To avoid decisions just to be safe and take no risks is to limit our experiences and avoid new learning.

Time Robs Us of Choice

We all feel that we don't have time to make choices in life. It seems there are so many commitments and obligations. Yet the truth is we all have the same amount of time to do the things we want to do. We have to identify what we will do and commit to it, conserving time for our chosen purposes and eliminating the distractions for each 24-hour day and 168-hour week.

Lost yesterday, somewhere between sunrise and sunset, two golden hours—each set with sixty diamond minutes. No reward is offered, as they are gone forever.
—Horace Mann

Certain personalities particularly struggle with the time problem. Let's look at them.

The Overorganizer

This person is always making lists and plans. He or she schedules a time slot for everything, then needs to keep track of everything on the list. Rarely does the overorganizer eliminate items that are old, have lost their value or are just low priority. He or she is too busy to take the time to reevaluate.

We shape our dwellings and then our dwellings shape us.
—Winston Churchill

The People Pleaser

When you need to make a choice and do not make it, that is a choice.

—William Joyce

This person avoids choices that will upset someone else. For any number of reasons, people pleasers feel that they cannot follow their own plans and dreams because someone else will be disappointed, hurt or even angry. Making choices then becomes too risky and the people pleaser forfeits his or her freedom.

It's just possible that you will have more time each week if you reevaluate how you spend your time now and make different choices. Ask yourself whether these time robbers are cheating you out of a more power-full life:

- Do I really have to go out to lunch every day, or can I prepare healthful small snacks and deal with hunger, health and time?
- Is there a possibility of turning off the TV one hour earlier or getting up one hour earlier and adding an hour to do something I really want to do?
- Do I need to answer every home phone or cell phone call that I get? Could I take voice mails and answer them in a block of time that I'm willing to devote to phone calls. Are there some calls I can choose to ignore?
- Is there a hobby, activity or pastime in my life that I can bring to a conclusion? Can I thank it for bringing me pleasure and then let it go? Have I outgrown some of my interests? There might be some extra hours per week for new interests if I were to let an old one go.

Rule of Five

One of the tools that has helped me most has been the "rule of five." On my desk I keep five boxes that contain important items. The boxes are labeled in order of importance—"number one" being the most important and "number five" the least. When mail comes in, I immediately sort it and put it in one of the five boxes, depending on importance. Bills always go into number one. As phone messages come in that don't require an immediate response, I put them in the appropriate box. As commitments and duties surface, I do the same. As ideas pop into my head, I also do the same.

> *Life is what we make it. This is how things have always been and how they will be until the end of time.*
>
> —*Grandma Moses*

Once a week, I tackle my boxes. I do number one right away. As I have the time, I then do numbers two through four. Anything in box number five is ignored and thrown away. In the beginning, it was hard to postpone boxes three and four and to ignore box five. But it got easier and easier. Finally, I have some time to call my own.

Controlling Communications

The second best tool is to know when to ignore certain phone calls and e-mails. Nobody said we have to be slaves to communication. I still want to have my choices. If I believe a call or an e-mail is important, I respond right away. I answer other calls and e-mails at my convenience or not at all. I choose not to be a communication junkie.

Simplify (Good, Better and Best)

I once asked three of my mentors the most important change or choice that a person could make concerning time management. All three said, "Simplify, simplify, simplify." One way to do that is to apply the "good, better, best" principle. When our choices in life are between good things and bad things, choosing the good over the bad is easy and usually makes things better. However, new choices then present themselves and those choices are between good and better. We now have to let some good things go in order to have better things! Later, new choices present themselves again, and we have to let some better things go in order to have the best choices. Now we arrive at a time when all our choices are between the best and best that there is.

We must be willing to get rid of the life we've planned so as to have the life that is waiting for us.

—Joseph Campbell

We cannot get to the point where all our choices are between the best and the best unless we are willing to let some good and better things go. As my good friend Lee Silverstein wrote: "At times, I found myself submerged, not by distractions, but by opportunities; not just by dull people, but by too many interesting people." Our lives can become crowded and hectic by wonderful people, events and circumstances. We may have to eliminate some good things just to find peace, quiet and rejuvenation.

If we refuse to make choices and refuse to simplify our lives, we will become drained and unable to enjoy all the wonderful things offered to us. Making choices is not for sissies or the weak. It is a demanding and risky job.

Feeling Stuck and Getting Free

When we feel overwhelmed and stuck in our lives, it's often because we are having trouble sorting out our values, our problems and our choices. The two charts that follow will help clarify what you truly value and highlight the areas of your life that need to change and heal.

First let's work with the Value Chart. Review the example provided, then go to the blank chart and list all the major areas of your life that you value. Look at the percentages—zero to 100 percent—listed on the side. Place a dot at the percentage you believe represents how each value harmonizes and is in balance with your life. For example, if you feel your work is in seventy-five percent harmony with your life, place a dot on the chart to indicate that.

Now, connect the dots. The space below the dotted line represents satisfaction and balance and illustrates where your behavior matches your stated value. The space above the dotted line represents areas of stress and where you need to change.

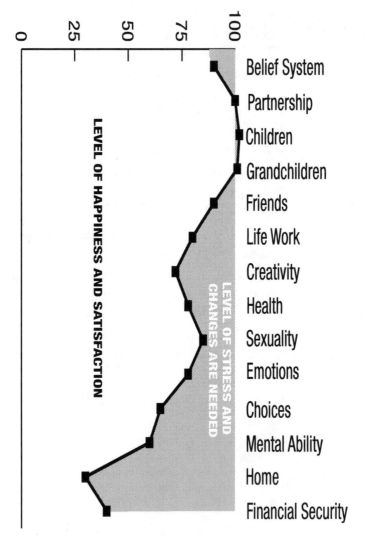

Value Chart

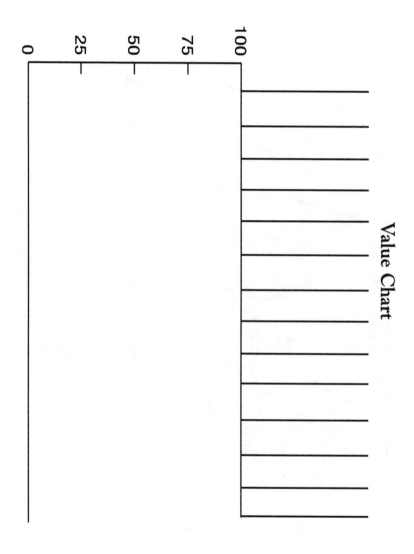

Value Chart

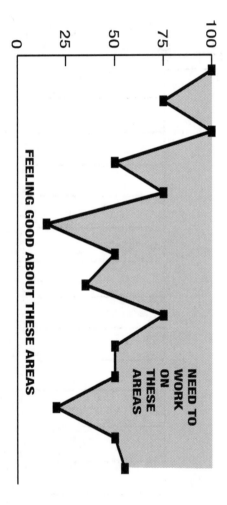

Problem Chart

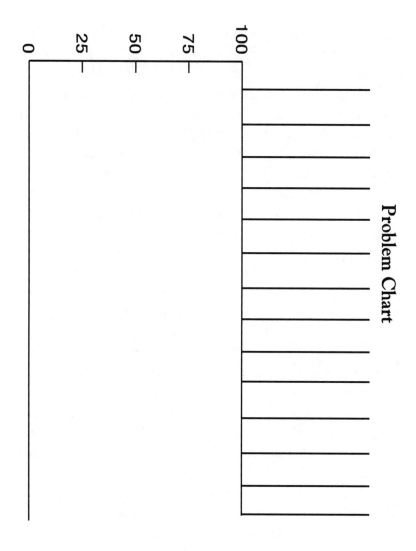

Problem Chart

The Problem Chart works the same way as the Value Chart. It further breaks down the problem areas of your life to help you see what you need to change.

Using the example as a guide, use the blank chart to list the issues that represent problem areas in your life. (I have listed the ones I see most often in the people I work with). Using the percentages listed on the side, place a dot at the percentage that represents your level of satisfaction about how you're dealing with a particular problem. For example, if you are struggling with compulsive eating, you would place your dot in the lower percentage area. The closer you are to 100 percent satisfied in your life, the less work you have to do in that area. The closer you are to zero percent indicates areas where you need to focus your attention and take action to become free of the problem.

Finding One's Way

Once we know our values, make choices and act to move ahead in areas where we're stuck, we can see more clearly both our strengths and our limitations. In knowing and accepting our own choices and the challenges that they bring, we can become much more accepting of others' differences as well. We recognize that they, too, are living their own truths. We are able to stop judging others and accept them for who they are.

Life gets easier when we decide to take charge of ourselves. Our fears of being controlled and losing ourselves evaporate because we now know we can make choices on our own behalf.

Helpful Reading

The One Minute Manager, Blanchard & Johnson, 1981.

The Sedona Method, Hale Dwoskin, Sedona Press, 2003.

How To Get Control of Your Time and Your Life, Alan Lakein, Signet, 1973.

The Choice, Og Mandino, Bantam Books, 1986.

Choicemaking, Sharon Wegscheider-Cruse, Deerfield Beach, FL: Health Communications, 1985.

Will Power Generators: Homework

- **Decide** on three things that you want to change and take the first step toward each goal. List the steps:

  1. _____

     _____

     _____

  2. _____

     _____

     _____

  3. _____

     _____

     _____

- **Simplify** an area of your life. Identify the area and indicate how you will simplify it.

  _____

  _____

  _____

  _____

  _____

- **Capture** one extra hour per day by changing something. How can you do this?

  _____

  _____

  _____

  _____

• **Say** "no" in one area of your life. Where will you do this?

_____

_____

_____

_____

_____

Will Power Journal   Week # ____

Can I make decisions easily?

_____

_____

_____

_____

_____

Am I willing to confront someone when necessary?

_____

_____

_____

_____

Am I supportive when the situation calls for support?

_____

_____

_____

_____

Am I open to change and new directions?

_____

_____

_____

_____

Am I willing to take important risks?

_____

_____

_____

_____

_____

Do I tend to procrastinate?

_____

_____

_____

_____

_____

Will Power Journal   Week # ____

Can I make decisions easily?

_____

_____

_____

_____

_____

Am I willing to confront someone when necessary?

_____

_____

_____

_____

Am I supportive when the situation calls for support?

_____

_____

_____

_____

Am I open to change and new directions?

_____

_____

_____

_____

Am I willing to take important risks?

_____

_____

_____

_____

_____

Do I tend to procrastinate?

_____

_____

_____

_____

_____

Will Power Journal   Week # ____

Can I make decisions easily?

_____

_____

_____

_____

_____

Am I willing to confront someone when necessary?

_____

_____

_____

_____

Am I supportive when the situation calls for support?

_____

_____

_____

_____

Am I open to change and new directions?

_____

_____

_____

_____

Am I willing to take important risks?

_____

_____

_____

_____

_____

Do I tend to procrastinate?

_____

_____

_____

_____

_____

Will Power Journal   Week # ____

Can I make decisions easily?

_____

_____

_____

_____

Am I willing to confront someone when necessary?

_____

_____

_____

_____

Am I supportive when the situation calls for support?

_____

_____

_____

_____

Am I open to change and new directions?

_____

_____

_____

_____

Am I willing to take important risks?

_____

_____

_____

_____

_____

Do I tend to procrastinate?

_____

_____

_____

_____

_____

Will Power Journal   Week # ____

Can I make decisions easily?

_____

_____

_____

_____

_____

Am I willing to confront someone when necessary?

_____

_____

_____

_____

_____

Am I supportive when the situation calls for support?

_____

_____

_____

_____

_____

Am I open to change and new directions?

_____

_____

_____

_____

_____

Am I willing to take important risks?

_____

_____

_____

_____

_____

Do I tend to procrastinate?

_____

_____

_____

_____

_____

Will Power Journal   Week # ____

Can I make decisions easily?

_____
_____
_____
_____

Am I willing to confront someone when necessary?

_____
_____
_____
_____

Am I supportive when the situation calls for support?

_____
_____
_____
_____

Am I open to change and new directions?

_____
_____
_____
_____

Am I willing to take important risks?

_____
_____

_____

_____

_____

Do I tend to procrastinate?

_____

_____

_____

_____

_____

Will Power Journal   Week # ____

Can I make decisions easily?

_____

_____

_____

_____

_____

Am I willing to confront someone when necessary?

_____

_____

_____

_____

Am I supportive when the situation calls for support?

_____

_____

_____

_____

Am I open to change and new directions?

_____

_____

_____

_____

Am I willing to take important risks?

_____

_____

_____

_____

_____

Do I tend to procrastinate?

_____

_____

_____

_____

_____

Will Power Journal   Week # ____

Can I make decisions easily?

_____

_____

_____

_____

_____

Am I willing to confront someone when necessary?

_____

_____

_____

_____

_____

Am I supportive when the situation calls for support?

_____

_____

_____

_____

_____

Am I open to change and new directions?

_____

_____

_____

_____

_____

Am I willing to take important risks?

_____

_____

_____

_____

_____

Do I tend to procrastinate?

_____

_____

_____

_____

_____

Will Power Journal   Week # ____

Can I make decisions easily?

_____

_____

_____

_____

_____

Am I willing to confront someone when necessary?

_____

_____

_____

_____

_____

Am I supportive when the situation calls for support?

_____

_____

_____

_____

_____

Am I open to change and new directions?

_____

_____

_____

_____

_____

Am I willing to take important risks?

_____

_____

_____

_____

_____

Do I tend to procrastinate?

_____

_____

_____

_____

_____

3

SPIRITUAL POWER

There must be more to life than having everything.

Maurice Sendak

Recovery of the Soul

The definition of "soul" includes many elements: our essence, spiritual core, emotional nature, vitality, substance, personality, force, honor, sense of beauty.

No matter which description fits your meaning of soul, it is a crucial part of who you are. It is in discovering your connection to your soul that you find your truth and your direction for your individual life.

The door to the soul opens inward because our truth lies within. We need to go inside ourselves and find out who we really are. We need to strip away all the outside protective shell and find our personal, delicate, yet power-full soul inside, waiting to be understood and expressed. The stripping away of our outside defenses is a challenge in itself. It means we stop responding to outside pressures and environments and begin listening to our own inside and intuitive self. This is not always easy. The older we are and the more fixed we are in our conditioning, the more protective shell there is. But there is no other way to go within.

> *Goodness is more important than wisdom and recognizing this is the beginning of wisdom.*
>
> —*Theodore Isaac Rubin*

> *Learn to get in touch with the silence within yourself and know that everything in this life has a purpose.*
>
> —*Elisabeth Kübler-Ross*

Many people can strip away their outside shell all by themselves and do a good job of it. Others need to have support to do this and work with a friend or a group of friends. Others, especially those who have suffered a major loss or series of losses, may need a therapist or counselor to help them remove the shell. This shell can be a great defense,

---

Spiritual Power: Signs of a Power Outage

(check any that apply)

__ I often feel that life is meaningless.

__ I am convinced that my spiritual beliefs are the only right ones.

__ I feel little or no responsibility to contribute to other people or to the world in general.

__ I often feel disappointed by my life.

__ I feel that life has been unfair to me.

__ I feel hopeless and helpless much of the time.

__ I resist the idea of a power outside of myself (a higher power).

__ I have bad or unfinished feelings about my religious upbringing.

__ I fear my future.

__ I often feel like nothing matters.

---

helping to protect a delicate soul and a hurting heart. But it also locks in a person's truth.

Hole in the Soul

When someone suffers what can be called a *hole in the soul*, he or she will develop a shell over that hole to prevent further loss and pain. There are many reasons people develop a hole in their soul:

- growing up in a painful family
- suffering a significant chronic illness

- a loved one with an addiction, such as to alcohol, gambling, sex, work, busyness, medication, etc.
- a partner who has had an affair
- the death of a significant person

> *Happiness isn't getting what you want, it's wanting what you have.*
>
> —*Anonymous*

Perhaps one of the most difficult reasons to understand is what I call *the void*. The void is not an overt trauma. It's an emptiness. People with an internal void just drift through life without a plan and with no sense of excitement or hope. They function, do the mundane things that must be done (eat, sleep, go to school, have a job), but there is no real purpose to their lives. They do not experience joy, accomplishment, creativity, etc. Parents or partners may provide shelter, clothing, education and social life, but no one has shown this person the way to his or her soul, or how to look inside oneself and discover one's own truth. This is a major loss for such a person, and he or she develops a shell to protect against any outside influence and to allow him or her to simply exist.

> *I have always said the people who do best in life are the ones with one hand reaching for angels and two feet firmly planted in the practical day-to-day life.*
>
> —*Anonymous*

People with a hole in their soul have a restlessness that can become self-destructive. They keep trying to fill their souls with substances and activities, but it doesn't work. They use money, fame, sex, work, gambling, sports, alcohol, nicotine, drugs or excessive exercise to try to fill the hole, but it just gets bigger.

The solution to uncovering souls buried under a shell or releasing locked-in truth or fixing a hole in the soul lies in transforming our lives through spiritual power. We must not confuse *spiritual power* with religious power. They are not the same. Webster's dictionary helps us understand the difference. It defines *religious* as "relating to a faithful devotion to an acknowledged ultimate reality or deity," while defining *spiritual* as "of the spirit or the soul." Every religion is spiritual, but not all spirituality is religious.

> *The day will come when after harnessing the winds, the tides and gravitation, we shall harness for God the energies of love—and on that day, for the second time in the history of the world, man will have discovered fire.*
>
> —*Teilhard de Chardin*

Spirituality has its roots deep in our universal human need to understand the meaning of life. It seeks answers to fundamental questions. Where have we come from? Why are we here? Where does our journey lead, and is someone orchestrating it all? What is the spirit of love and goodness between humans? What is the value system we develop for ourselves?

Spiritual power helps us ask questions and find answers that ring true for each of us. The answers become our truth.

Each person and each generation must discover their own paths to and versions of spiritual connection, which is why the forms of spiritual searching are always changing, although the process remains constant.

The possibilities of exploration go beyond the mundane aspects of life and infuse it with an awareness and light that give meaning, beauty and sense to our individual lives. Spiritual power gives us the means to find inner peace and happiness in an imperfect world. Spiritual power can simply mean having the ability to love, to experience and to deepen our sensitivity to life.

Knowing Who We Are

Knowing our truth and acting honestly on that knowledge is a big challenge. So often we are defined by what family, friends, professions and society expect of us. We become slaves to the expectations we have for ourselves or others have for us. We take few risks, and we do little soul searching.

> *It is a mistake to look too far ahead. Only one link in the chain of destiny can be handled at a time.*
>
> —*Winston Churchill*

If we examine ourselves, we often do not know what we truly believe. We need to discover what is so important that not only are we willing to die for it, but we are also willing *to live for it.* When we know and describe that value, we have a plan for our lives. Albert Einstein said, "The minute you begin to live your life according to your choices, it's really a new kind of life."

The energy is there for all of us to live this new life of spiritual simplicity. By this, I don't mean a sackcloth, weak broth and denying the pleasures of the world. Using God's gifts can be a spiritual happening. Living spiritually means living with attitudes and values of simplicity. It means moving from:

- restlessness to focus and gratitude
- self-interest to meaning outside of ourselves
- resentment to acceptance
- dishonesty to honesty
- depression to joy
- lethargy to action
- powerlessness to power
- indecision to decision

Spiritual transformation and discovering our truth comes about naturally when we consistently place our trust in a higher power. For those who are open to meaning, experience tends to teach us that there is a higher or universal power that is a loving and creative energy in each person's life, a divine protection. People can experience and come to trust this higher power in many different ways:

- by intuitive understanding
- through apparent coincidences in life events that affect us deeply
- by the intricate and infinite complexity and inter-dependence of life
- through the unconditional love of another person

This power outside us, which paradoxically becomes available to each of us when we look inside, gives us tools to care for ourselves and fosters compassion to help and care for others. We develop a desire to make this world a better place for others and ourselves.

I have been asked many times how I would define "spirituality." What feels like the clearest definition to me is the relationship between me and me, me and you, and me and my higher power. When I am honest and clear with myself, then I can relate to you, my higher power and those around me. When all those relationships are in sync, then there is a power and energy released that is healing for me and for others.

Giving money isn't enough. Money can always be found. What the poor need is love. Spread love wherever your path takes you. Many persons strive for high ideas and everywhere life is full of heroism. In the noisy confusion of life, keep peace with your soul.

—Desiderata

German dramatist Christian Friedrich Habble said, "Life is not anything. It is only the opportunity for something." Living a spiritual life is an opportunity. We give our spirit fullest expression when we choose to live a full life and make the most of it. Helen Keller put it this way: "Life is either a daring adventure or nothing." To pursue a spiritual path is the most daring of all adventures.

Spiritually Hungry Vagabonds

Most of us find it all too easy to get caught up in mundane concerns: the next big success at work, prestige, power, old hurts, current comforts, new ways to get high and excited, day-to-day worries, cleaning the house, cooking dinner and helping with homework, among others.

It's just as easy to get caught up in distractions while pursuing the spiritual path. The spiritually hungry seek out new gurus and another round of theories to help them find either excitement or peace. Apart from momentary releases and insights, however, they remain hungry and unfilled. Sometimes they become "theory vagabonds," moving from one set of ideas and beliefs to another.

The spiritually hungry resist looking inward and listening to their experience and what they know to be true. They resist trusting in a power outside themselves. And they resist taking the actions and making the changes and choices that need to be made so they can love, commit and act in a way that brings about personal fulfillment and joy in their relationships.

Altered-State Junkies

Another distraction from spiritual development is to become an "altered-state junkie" who continually seeks out exotic new highs and finds more and more ways to avoid his or her own truth. Healthy living can seem mundane to the person who is spiritually bankrupt and who constantly short circuits attempts to establish a sustained spiritual energy connection. Intermittent flashes of insight and jolts of ecstatic feeling without a solid grounding ultimately become an energy drain.

Healthy living has a sense of inner peace about it. It's a quiet fulfillment that leads to feelings of comfort, ease and acceptance. Sometimes healthy people even seem a bit boring to those who are always looking for excitement and action. When people are spiritually bankrupt, they have few inner resources to bring them satisfaction and fulfillment. They then look to something external to make them feel better. It might be excitement, newness or action of some sort. They want a new sport, a new partner, a new venture, etc. The temporary rush of excitement masks the true hunger for contentment and peace. In this way, seeking an altered state becomes a desperate attempt to feel normal. This is what I mean by an "altered-state junkie."

Soul Mates

Constantly searching for a perfect partner to fix our problems is also a distraction on the spiritual path. When people are not at home in their own souls and are unaware or afraid of their truth, they sometimes look to others to spark them into feeling connected. It's another attempt to fill the hole in the soul. It never works. These people serially connect with partners or mates and continually find dissatisfaction. They will go from relationship to relationship, each time believing that this is the one that will work. Some leave marriages and others have affairs, yet the pattern—and the result—is the same: excitement, hope, disappointment, anger and remorse.

This pattern will keep recurring until people find their own souls. Then they will be capable of finding partners who have discovered their own souls, and they can become *soul mates,* helping each other develop spirituality together. All other relationships will ultimately feel lonely and unsatisfying.

Excess Baggage: Who Needs It?

Carrying excess baggage also impedes connecting with our spiritual power. The baggage can take many forms: too many unresolved emotions, too many material goods, too much money, too many relationships, too many goals, too many decisions, too many commitments. In spiritual transformation, we learn that we must risk leaving behind the baggage that weighs us down. Until we let go, we remain encumbered. As the medieval theologian Meister Eckhart observed, "The soul does not grow by addition, but by subtraction."

When we are able to let go, to calm ourselves, to ignore the clamor of the newest spiritual fad, we start to become aware of our truth and our message. And the clues, teachers and events that confirm our message come to us unbidden.

It can be so frightening to simply trust and wait. We want to make things happen. Although we may consciously know that ships come in on calm and supporting seas, we often keep the waters churning and stormy. It is our job to get ready for the messages and the transformations. Getting ready and being "in waiting" is the very difficult, active work we have to do to connect with our spiritual power. It is like waiting for the reservoir to fill with the water that will drive the turbines in a hydroelectric dam. When there is enough water, the power flows with no effort.

Angels: Have One or Be One

Spiritual power also enables us to see the angels in our lives. Angels are those people who the higher power uses to bring new messages to others. We all know about the angels in our lives. There is that person who is always there for us, ready to listen to us and support us when we need it, and also ready to play when we need play in our lives. Angels stand by and seem to know what we need and give it to us. Angels come in two spiritual guises—mentors and teachers. Mentors show the way and support us; teachers confront, challenge and push us through struggles. Angels appear in the bodily form of parents, children, other family, educators and close friends. Sometimes angels even appear as strangers. We know when we have been around an angel because we feel good about ourselves.

I have a friend who makes me laugh. She is a busy woman, and we don't see each other often. However, she has this way about her that allows her to look at life as a joyful place. Together we seem to see the funny side of things. We laugh a lot when we are together. Some say laughter is exercise for the soul. My friend is an angel to me, and she keeps my soul in shape.

One of my most dramatic angel moments occurred when I was speaking to an audience of a thousand people. At a certain moment in my presentation, I announced that I was going to play the song "Amazing Grace." The lights were dimmed, the audience was silent, I pressed the button on the tape recorder—and nothing happened. I panicked and pressed the button again. Still nothing happened. I stopped breathing and pressed the button one more time. Nothing! Before I could find my voice to say anything to the audience, there was a rustle as a man came onto the stage and went to a keyboard behind me. He began to play "Amazing Grace," as if that was how it had been planned. That chance meeting introduced me to Jerry Florence of the musical group Go with the Flow. Jerry became a dear friend and, subsequently, brought his music and traveled with my soul mate Joe Cruse, and me for many years. He was a true angel in our lives.

Prophets and Modern-Day Messengers

People charged with spiritual power can also tune in to the prophets and messengers in our midst, who I consider divinely inspired. There have been divine prophets and messengers throughout history, and I believe that they are still here in our everyday lives. We only need to recognize them in one another. Perhaps we each have the possibility of becoming a spiritually charged messenger. Perhaps a prophet is one who is simply inspired by his or her own life of prayer and action. If that is so, we only need to listen to one another and learn one another's truth. Perhaps the greatest way to connect with a higher power is to listen to those that we admire and love.

Meditation and Prayer: Energy Sources

Our spiritual power comes from within. We only need to tap into it. One of the ways we can do that is to pray and meditate, which completes the circuit with our higher power and connects us with the spiritual energy grid that encircles the world and links all people.

Often, prayer is called asking the higher power for guidance, and meditation is described as listening for the response. Prayer and meditation come in many forms:

- listening to music
- reading inspirational books
- spending time in nature
- looking for the good in others
- sharing romance with a soul mate
- enjoying beauty in any form
- simply being awed by life's mystery and magic

In describing this gift of prayer, I am not saying that we always feel vibrant, confidant and upbeat. Even the most spiritually empowered and faithful have blackouts and feel disconnected from any spiritual energy. But with faith, we also have resilience and can draw on reserves of courage, hope and strength when we need it.

Because our spiritual power is generated from within, it is not patched on from an outer source. We stop looking for answers outside of ourselves. As we come to know and accept our truth, more and more of our inner spirit is released. We are each leading the lives we are supposed to live. We are each simply *a link* in the unbroken chain of spirit that connects all things. We need to ask ourselves what and who are we holding together, and are we doing our part? Knowing and accepting our role as a link is a very important part of knowing who we are and what our purpose is in life.

Helpful Reading

The Five People You Meet In Heaven, Mitch Albom, Hyperion, 2003.

The Healing Dimensions, Brent Baum, West Press, 1997.

Healers on Healing, Richard Carlson and Benjamin Shield, Jeremy Tarcher/Putnam, 1989.

The Thirst for Wholeness, Christina Grof, Harper Collins, 1993.

When All You've Ever Wanted Isn't Enough, Harold Kushner, Simon & Schuster, 1965.

The Care of The Soul, Thomas Moore, HarperPerennial, 1994.

The Four Agreements, Don Miguel Ruiz, Amber-Allen Publishing, Inc., 1997.

The Voice of Knowledge, Don Miguel Ruiz, Amber-Allen Publishing, Inc., 2004.

Spiritual Power Generators: Homework

- **Listen** to the angels in your life and the people you truly respect. Find your prophets. List some of them here:

  _____

  _____

  _____

  _____

  _____

- **Become** an angel and a messenger to someone else. When we listen carefully, all people have the chance to become teachers. Who are some of the people you would like to become an angel to?

  _____

  _____

  _____

  _____

  Who have been some of the angels in your life?

  _____

  _____

  _____

  _____

- **Meditate.** Spend time alone without distraction and hear your inner self offering ideas and inspiration When we mediate, we become creative. Where (in your home) will you meditate? _____

What tools will you use to help you in your plans to meditate?

_____

_____

_____

_____

_____

- **Pray.** As we pray, we go into action. We can offer our services and become part of the group that makes this world a better place to live. We can donate, volunteer or join groups, committees and boards. We can choose to live more fully in the world and make our corner of it better. What does prayer mean to you?

_____

_____

_____

_____

_____

Spiritual Power Journal   Week # ____

Do I have a sense of meaning in my life?

_____

_____

_____

_____

_____

_____

Do I feel connected to anything more than just myself?

_____

_____

_____

_____

_____

_____

Do I accept and have faith in other people?

_____

_____

_____

_____

_____

_____

READER/CUSTOMER CARE SURVEY

HEFG

We care about your opinions! Please take a moment to fill out our online Reader Survey at **http://survey.hcibooks.com**.
As a **"THANK YOU"** you will receive a **VALUABLE INSTANT COUPON** towards future book purchases as well as a **SPECIAL GIFT** available
only online! Or, you may mail this card back to us and we will send you a copy of our exciting catalog with your valuable coupon inside.
(PLEASE PRINT IN ALL CAPS)

First Name _____ MI. _____ Last Name _____

Address _____

State _____ Zip _____ City _____ Email: _____

1. Gender
❏ Female   ❏ Male

2. Age
❏ 8 or younger
❏ 9-12   ❏ 13-16
❏ 17-20   ❏ 21-30
❏ 31+

3. Did you receive this book as a gift?
❏ Yes   ❏ No

4. Annual Household Income
❏ under $25,000
❏ $25,000 - $34,999
❏ $35,000 - $49,999
❏ $50,000 - $74,999
❏ over $75,000

5. What are the ages of the children living in your house
❏ 0 - 14   ❏ 15+

6. Marital Status
❏ Single
❏ Married
❏ Divorced
❏ Widowed

7. How did you find out about the book
(please choose one)
❏ Recommendation
❏ Store Display
❏ Online
❏ Catalog/Mailing
❏ Interview/Review

8. Where do you usually buy books
(please choose one)
❏ Bookstore
❏ Online
❏ Book Club/Mail Order
❏ Price Club (Sam's Club, Costco's, etc.)
❏ Retail Store (Target, Wal-Mart, etc.)

9. What subject do you enjoy reading about the most
(please choose one)
❏ Parenting/Family
❏ Relationships
❏ Recovery/Addictions
❏ Health/Nutrition
❏ Christianity
❏ Spirituality/Inspiration
❏ Business Self-help
❏ Women's Issues
❏ Sports

10. What attracts you most to a book
(please choose one)
❏ Title
❏ Cover Design
❏ Author
❏ Content

TAPE IN MIDDLE; DO NOT STAPLE

BUSINESS REPLY MAIL
FIRST-CLASS MAIL PERMIT NO 45 DEERFIELD BEACH, FL

POSTAGE WILL BE PAID BY ADDRESSEE

Health Communications, Inc.
3201 SW 15th Street
Deerfield Beach FL 33442-9875

FOLD HERE

Comments

Do I have a sense of inner peace and hope for my future?

_____

_____

_____

_____

_____

_____

_____

Do I have a form of meditation and prayer that is important to me?

_____

_____

_____

_____

_____

_____

_____

Can I articulate my values?

_____

_____

_____

_____

_____

_____

_____

Spiritual Power Journal   Week # ____

Do I have a sense of meaning in my life?

_____

_____

_____

_____

_____

_____

_____

Do I feel connected to anything more than just myself?

_____

_____

_____

_____

_____

_____

_____

Do I accept and have faith in other people?

_____

_____

_____

_____

_____

_____

_____

Do I have a sense of inner peace and hope for my future?

_____

_____

_____

_____

_____

_____

_____

Do I have a form of meditation and prayer that is important to me?

_____

_____

_____

_____

_____

_____

Can I articulate my values?

_____

_____

_____

_____

_____

_____

Spiritual Power Journal   Week # ____

Do I have a sense of meaning in my life?

_____

_____

_____

_____

_____

_____

Do I feel connected to anything more than just myself?

_____

_____

_____

_____

_____

_____

Do I accept and have faith in other people?

_____

_____

_____

_____

_____

_____

Do I have a sense of inner peace and hope for my future?

_____

_____

_____

_____

_____

_____

_____

Do I have a form of meditation and prayer that is important
to me?

_____

_____

_____

_____

_____

_____

_____

Can I articulate my values?

_____

_____

_____

_____

_____

_____

_____

Spiritual Power Journal   Week # ____

Do I have a sense of meaning in my life?

_____

_____

_____

_____

_____

_____

_____

Do I feel connected to anything more than just myself?

_____

_____

_____

_____

_____

_____

Do I accept and have faith in other people?

_____

_____

_____

_____

_____

_____

Do I have a sense of inner peace and hope for my future?

_____

_____

_____

_____

_____

_____

_____

Do I have a form of meditation and prayer that is important to me?

_____

_____

_____

_____

_____

_____

Can I articulate my values?

_____

_____

_____

_____

_____

_____

4

EMOTIONAL POWER

*T*rust in the invisible force of feelings. They know more than your brain could ever know about making your dreams come true.

Joseph Bailey

The Walking Dead

There is a difference between walking through life fully alive and vibrant and getting through life on automatic pilot—which is akin to being among the walking dead. Your body is alive, but your heart and soul are numb.

> *The pain of losing a loved one is the price we pay for having had that love.*
>
> —Evelyn Underhill

Part of finding our balance is to be able to feel, name and express our feelings. Feelings are not right or wrong. They just are. Feelings are also a form of energy. That is why our feelings are a big part of who we are. When you burn your finger, you feel pain. When you watch the birth of a child, you feel awe. When someone points a gun at you, you feel fear. When someone says that they love you, you feel joy.

There is a range of more than one hundred feelings available to us, and as we allow ourselves to feel all of them, we come closer to our truth. Feelings give us emotional power.

Fear of Feeling

Some people fear their own feelings. They do not want to ever feel pain, hurt, sadness, loneliness, emptiness, guilt, shame, anger, embarrassment—or even fear itself. They create a coat of armor around them for protection. The problem with this armor is that it also blocks joy, excitement, happiness,

> *The booze that leaves you breathless also can leave you careless, homeless, family-less and jobless.*
>
> —Lee Silverstein

Emotional Power: Signs of a Power Outage

(check any that apply)

___ I often medicate my feelings with excess food.

___ I sometimes medicate my feelings with excess alcohol.

___ I sometimes medicate my feelings with drugs.

___ I often medicate my feelings by smoking cigarettes.

___ I medicate my feelings with excess work and/or activity.

___ I sometimes medicate my feelings by sexual acting out.

___ I often medicate my feelings by gambling.

___ I sometimes medicate my feelings with excess exercise.

___ I often feel depressed.

___ I have difficulty expressing my emotions when it comes to anger, hurt, jealousy, embarrassment or sadness.

___ I keep my feelings inside about my family, partner, past family or coworkers.

curiosity and love. Our truth includes all feelings, not just the ones we want to have.

To avoid feeling, some people medicate themselves with alcohol, drugs, cigarettes, gambling, sex, work, exercise, busyness, controlling or overresponsibility. The more they medicate, the harder it becomes to know themselves and to connect with someone who is able to feel.

Feeling Versus Intellect

In this era of information overload, with an endless stream of e-mail, Internet sites, books, magazines and television, we come to realize that information is not enough in our lives. We need to stop and feel. "Feeling" is the magic word. Feeling gives us a new energy.

We tend to overrate intellect and underrate feeling.

It is terribly amazing how many climates of feeling one can go through in a day.

—Anne Morrow Lindbergh

Intellect can lead to money, power and prestige. Emotion can lead to joy, excitement, happiness and hope. Yet it can also lead to vulnerability and anger, hurt, and guilt. Is it any wonder that feelings have sometimes gotten a bad rap?

But the reality that our intellect *perceives* to be true is open to interpretation. That reality can be misrepresented and misunderstood. While we readily acknowledge the importance of intellect, which I explore in the chapter on mental power, I believe that we must accept that emotions are equally important.

Relationship Complications

Expressing emotions is essential to healthy relationships. It is in the sharing of feelings that intimacy is developed. Intimacy is one of the greatest joys in life. It can exist in many different relationships, between lovers, between parents and children, and between friends.

Emotions do not lie. They tell our truth. When we share our truth with someone, we feel trust and closeness. As we understand the way feelings work, we can see how devastating smoking, drinking to excess, working to excess, sexual affairs, excess gambling and excess eating can be to relationships. Those behaviors effectively deny people their feelings. In our culture, it is easy to medicate feelings. Medicated or repressed feelings become blocked. *You can't heal what you can't feel, and you can't feel what you medicate.*

Not only are chemical and behavioral medications successful in denying access to feelings, they also bring about complications in lives and relationships that bring more pain and hurt. This, in turn, leads people to continue medicating with chemicals or behavior and creates a vicious cycle.

> *Happiness consists of living each day as if it were the first day of your honeymoon and the last day of your vacation.*
>
> —*Anonymous*

> *Cancer is a high price to pay to solve problems that could be solved instead by altering your rules so that you give yourself permission to pay attention to your needs.*
>
> —*O. Carl Simonton, M.D.*

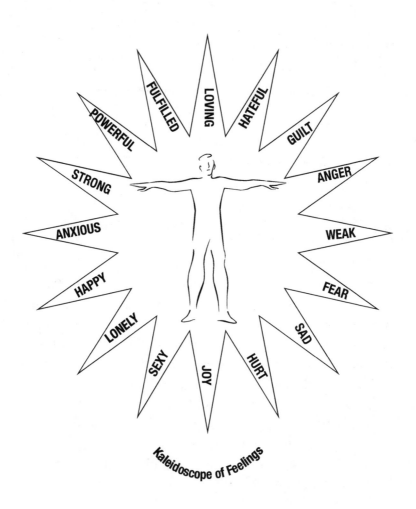

Kaleidoscope of Feelings

A Kaleidoscope of Emotions

There are no bad or negative feelings. All feelings have a purpose and a meaning. Think of them as displays of our energy level. Our range of feeling is enormous. Here are just a few of some of the familiar ways we can feel: happy, guilty, ashamed, excited, worried, resentful, grateful, interested, bored, ecstatic, afraid, silly, serious, eager, doomed, sexy, flat, sensual, strong or weak. Emotions will always tell us the truth.

Toxic People and Situations

When we are around toxic situations or toxic people, we may feel inadequate, afraid, cautious or uneasy. We can literally feel energy drain out of us, which tells us that this is not a safe place to be. When we are loved and cherished, we feel warm, safe, close and loving. We are infused with energy. We know that this is a situation or a person that we want to be around. When we have been praised or approved of, we feel self-acceptance and confidence. We literally beam with happiness or glow with pride.

If we do not express a feeling, it turns into a defense. This defense blocks further feelings that might be painful. In fact, defensive states are actually unexpressed feelings. Here are just a few examples of what unexpressed feelings become:

- Anger becomes depression.
- Fear becomes avoidance.
- Guilt becomes shame.
- Sadness becomes illness.
- Loneliness becomes aloneness.
- Boredom becomes restlessness.
- Inadequacy becomes low self-worth.

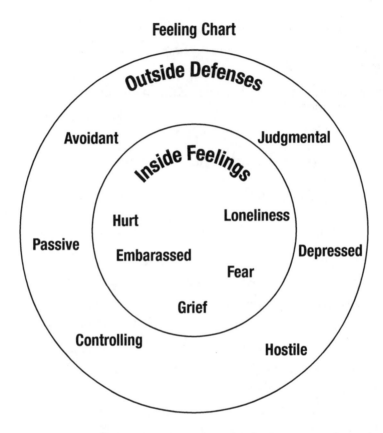

Feeling Chart

Medicators will keep painful feelings inside and
defensive attitudes will keep them there.

Recapturing Feelings:
Starting the Process

There are two stages to recapturing the power of
emotions. The first part is removing the medicating
offender, whether behavioral or chemical. The second
stage is letting the feelings surface and heal. Often our
early feelings in a situation will be fear, anger, anxiety,

shame and guilt. There is a sense that everything is falling apart. But as those emotions are felt and expressed, a healing will begin. Then feelings of relief, comfort, confidence and adequacy will start to surface.

Crying opens up the lungs, washes the countenance, exercises the eyes and softens the temper, so cry away.
—Charles Dickens

Sometimes people can navigate this whole process by themselves. Other times they may need some group support or professional guidance. Either way, they will need support from people around them, and it may be important to put together a "family of choice" that will support their efforts. A family of choice is a small group of four to six people who can be counted on at all times. They offer unconditional love.

Feelings and Health

There are many reasons to feel—beyond increasing the capacity to experience joy and establish intimacy. Feeling positive and hopeful when diagnosed with a disease can make a significant difference to healing. There is growing research evidence that a positive attitude toward treatment is a better predictor of response to treatment than is the severity of the disease. Some biologists go so far as to claim that when people feel and express their emotions, they feel more in control of their lives and in some ways are able to prevent certain diseases.

Helpful Reading

From Panic to Power, Lucinda Bassett, Harper Collins, 1995.

Grief Recovery Handbook, John W. James and Russell Friedan, Harper Perennial, 1998.

Full Catastrophe Living, Jon Kabat-Zinn, Dell Publishing, 1990.

I Exist, I Need, I'm Entitled, Jacqueline Lair and Walther Lechler, Doubleday, 1980.

The Dance of Anger, Harriet Lerner, Ph.D., Quill Publishing, 2001.

Understanding Your Immune System, Eve Potts and Marion Morray, Avon, 1986.

Emotionally Free, David Viscott, M.D., Contemporary Books, 1992.

Another Chance: Hope and Health for the Alcoholic Family, Sharon Wegscheider-Cruse, Science and Behavior Books (2nd edition), 1989.

The Heart of the Soul, Gary Zukav and Linda Francis, Simon & Schuster, 2002.

Emotional Power Generators: Homework

- **Stop** unnecessary medications and behaviors (nicotine, recreational drugs, alcohol abuse). Which of these medications have you used to avoid your feelings?

  _____

  _____

  _____

  _____

  _____

- **Modify** behaviors that medicate your natural emotions (overeating, sexual affairs, gambling, overworking, surfing the Internet, etc.). Which of these behaviors has been a problem for you?

  _____

  _____

  _____

  _____

  _____

- **Learn** more about the power of emotions. Join a group, read about feelings and emotional health, listen to music, experience movies, watch children play, etc. Pick one activity this week to expand your emotional self:

  _____

  _____

  _____

  _____

- **Allow** your feelings to surface and share them. Select one new activity or action this week and share your feelings about that activity or action with one person:

  _____

  _____

  _____

  _____

  _____

  _____

- **Express** your emotional truth. Choose a feeling that you don't usually share with anyone and share it with a trusted friend:

  _____

  _____

  _____

  _____

  _____

Emotional Power Journal   Week # ____

Am I aware of my feelings, and can I identify them?

_____

_____

_____

_____

_____

Am I able to express my feelings clearly and directly?

_____

_____

_____

_____

_____

Am I respectful of others' feelings, and do I listen?

_____

_____

_____

_____

_____

Have I eliminated all chemical medicators?

_____

_____

_____

_____

_____

Have I eliminated and/or modified behaviors that I have used to medicate feelings?

_____

_____

_____

_____

_____

Have I grieved my losses?

_____

_____

_____

_____

_____

Have I expressed anger where I need to?

_____

_____

_____

_____

_____

Do I know how to laugh and play on a regular basis?

_____

_____

_____

_____

_____

Emotional Power Journal   Week # ____

Am I aware of my feelings, and can I identify them?

_____

_____

_____

_____

_____

Am I able to express my feelings clearly and directly?

_____

_____

_____

_____

_____

Am I respectful of others' feelings, and do I listen?

_____

_____

_____

_____

_____

Have I eliminated all chemical medicators?

_____

_____

_____

_____

_____

Have I eliminated and/or modified behaviors that I have used to medicate feelings?

_____

_____

_____

_____

_____

Have I grieved my losses?

_____

_____

_____

_____

_____

Have I expressed anger where I need to?

_____

_____

_____

_____

_____

Do I know how to laugh and play on a regular basis?

_____

_____

_____

_____

_____

Emotional Power Journal   Week # ____

Am I aware of my feelings, and can I identify them?

_____

_____

_____

_____

_____

Am I able to express my feelings clearly and directly?

_____

_____

_____

_____

Am I respectful of others' feelings, and do I listen?

_____

_____

_____

_____

_____

Have I eliminated all chemical medicators?

_____

_____

_____

_____

Have I eliminated and/or modified behaviors that I have used to medicate feelings?

_____

_____

_____

_____

_____

Have I grieved my losses?

_____

_____

_____

_____

_____

Have I expressed anger where I need to?

_____

_____

_____

_____

_____

Do I know how to laugh and play on a regular basis?

_____

_____

_____

_____

_____

Emotional Power Journal   Week # ____

Am I aware of my feelings, and can I identify them?

_____

_____

_____

_____

_____

Am I able to express my feelings clearly and directly?

_____

_____

_____

_____

_____

Am I respectful of others' feelings, and do I listen?

_____

_____

_____

_____

_____

Have I eliminated all chemical medicators?

_____

_____

_____

_____

Have I eliminated and/or modified behaviors that I have used to medicate feelings?

_____

_____

_____

_____

_____

Have I grieved my losses?

_____

_____

_____

_____

_____

Have I expressed anger where I need to?

_____

_____

_____

_____

_____

Do I know how to laugh and play on a regular basis?

_____

_____

_____

_____

Emotional Power Journal   Week # ____

Am I aware of my feelings, and can I identify them?

_____

_____

_____

_____

_____

Am I able to express my feelings clearly and directly?

_____

_____

_____

_____

Am I respectful of others' feelings, and do I listen?

_____

_____

_____

_____

Have I eliminated all chemical medicators?

_____

_____

_____

_____

Have I eliminated and/or modified behaviors that I have used to medicate feelings?

_____

_____

_____

_____

_____

Have I grieved my losses?

_____

_____

_____

_____

Have I expressed anger where I need to?

_____

_____

_____

_____

Do I know how to laugh and play on a regular basis?

_____

_____

_____

_____

Emotional Power Journal   Week # ____

Am I aware of my feelings, and can I identify them?

_____

_____

_____

_____

_____

Am I able to express my feelings clearly and directly?

_____

_____

_____

_____

_____

Am I respectful of others' feelings, and do I listen?

_____

_____

_____

_____

_____

Have I eliminated all chemical medicators?

_____

_____

_____

_____

_____

Have I eliminated and/or modified behaviors that I have used to medicate feelings?

_____

_____

_____

_____

_____

Have I grieved my losses?

_____

_____

_____

_____

_____

Have I expressed anger where I need to?

_____

_____

_____

_____

_____

Do I know how to laugh and play on a regular basis?

_____

_____

_____

_____

_____

Emotional Power Journal   Week # ____

Am I aware of my feelings, and can I identify them?

_____

_____

_____

_____

_____

Am I able to express my feelings clearly and directly?

_____

_____

_____

_____

_____

Am I respectful of others' feelings, and do I listen?

_____

_____

_____

_____

_____

Have I eliminated all chemical medicators?

_____

_____

_____

_____

_____

Have I eliminated and/or modified behaviors that I have used to medicate feelings?

_____

_____

_____

_____

_____

Have I grieved my losses?

_____

_____

_____

_____

_____

Have I expressed anger where I need to?

_____

_____

_____

_____

_____

Do I know how to laugh and play on a regular basis?

_____

_____

_____

_____

_____

Emotional Power Journal   Week # ____

Am I aware of my feelings, and can I identify them?

_____

_____

_____

_____

_____

Am I able to express my feelings clearly and directly?

_____

_____

_____

_____

_____

Am I respectful of others' feelings, and do I listen?

_____

_____

_____

_____

_____

Have I eliminated all chemical medicators?

_____

_____

_____

_____

_____

Have I eliminated and/or modified behaviors that I have used to medicate feelings?

_____

_____

_____

_____

_____

Have I grieved my losses?

_____

_____

_____

_____

_____

Have I expressed anger where I need to?

_____

_____

_____

_____

_____

Do I know how to laugh and play on a regular basis?

_____

_____

_____

_____

_____

5

SOCIAL POWER

*G*o where you're celebrated, not tolerated.

Anonymous

Finding One's Way Through a Social Network

We all want and need caring relationships. We are social creatures who exchange energy. The better we are able to create and maintain relationships, the more social power we have—and the better we can interact with others.

> *We are born helpless. As soon as we are fully conscious we discover loneliness. We need others, physically, emotionally, intellectually—we need them if we are to know anything, even ourselves.*
>
> —*C.S. Lewis*

Sometimes we start out right in life and have cherished relationships that begin in our families. Many of us learned early on the art of walking through life connected to people we love and who love us. Others did not have such a great time of it. Their families were too busy. They struggled with time, money, alcohol, success and other types of stress. People from these families are often thrust into the world to figure relationships out for themselves.

Sometimes friends were the first people who taught us relationships could bring excitement, sharing, trust and possibility. During high school and college, we may form bonds that last many years, if not a lifetime.

Social Power: Signs of a Power Outage

(check any that apply)

__ I have broken trust in a relationship.

__ I spend too much time alone.

__ I spend too little time alone. (I am always available to others.)

__ My friendships are limited to coworkers.

__ I waste a lot of time (phone calls, e-mails, lunches) with people who are not important to me.

__ I do not have enough time for my primary relationship.

__ I do not have enough time for my current family.

__ I do not take time to honor relationships from my past.

__ I do not do my share in keeping up good friendships.

__ I am willing to be part of one-way relationships in which I do most of the work.

__ There is pain in many of my relationships.

These friendships often become increasingly important as we age. Then come the workplace, our early living situations and another group of people who become important to us. Whether it is the original family or high school, college or work friends that impact us the most, it's the people we surround ourselves with that set the pace and determine how many close relationships we have.

As an infant and young child, we have little choice about whom we want to be close to. However, as time progresses and we mature, we have more choice in this area. The people we choose to be part of the circle of support and love around us is our *"family of choice."* This is a fluid, ever changing mix of people, and it requires thought, work and decision making to develop and maintain this support system. There are layers of involvement. At any time, our support system may include family, coworkers and near or distant friends. A family of choice includes:

> *Call it a clan, call it a network, call it a tribe, call it a family . . . whatever you call it, whoever you are, you need one.*
>
> —Jane Howard

The Inner Circle

These are the people you are closest to. There are no secrets, and communication is honest, frequent and real. There is a free flow of emotional energy, and the exchange with these people is very valuable to your well-being. You are comfortable with confrontation and intimacy and together generate an environment that sustains mutual learning and trust. Usually a person can maintain only about ten of these inner-circle friends.

Golden Friends

These are people you choose to spend time with. They may live nearby so you can easily see them regularly, but even if they live at a distance, you make the effort to stay current and see them as often as you can.

You may agree or disagree about many things, but you ignore your differences because they do not matter as much as the closeness. Time with these people is valuable. You share a great deal together.

> *To have a friend takes time.*
>
> —Georgia O'Keeffe

Silver Friends

These are neighbors, club members and old high school and college friends with whom you have shared time in the past. You aren't intimate friends at this time, but you were once. These are the kind of friendships in which you pick up where you left off even if it was a long time ago. These are old connections with staying power.

Acquaintances

These are people you see regularly, know just a bit and have a pleasant, if low-powered, relationship with. They may be teachers, clergy, members of a sports team, a golf buddy, a fellow party invitee, a neighbor, a beautician, a personal trainer or a club member, among others.

Possibilities

These are people you have met—or have yet to meet—with whom you might develop a relationship. Remember that relationships are friendships with give and take, shared information, equal contribution and shared feelings, thoughts and ideas. The more you share your truth—your honesty and feelings—the more chance there is that a relationship will develop.

Relationship Chart:
Your Family of Choice

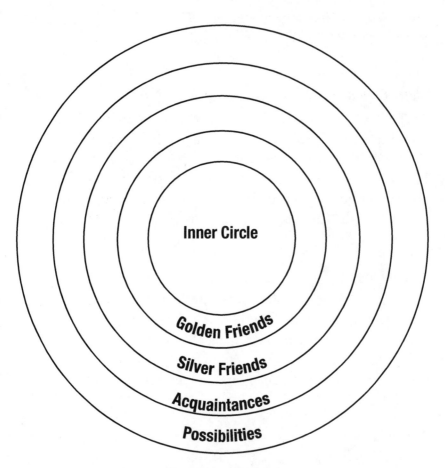

FILL IN NAMES IMPORTANT TO YOU

Choosing Our Closest Friends

It's easy to see we need to be mindful of our relationships. Each of us only has twenty-four hours to work with every day. We have to subtract time for sleeping, personal hygiene, eating and work, exercise and prayer and meditation right off the top. Then we deduct auto care, commuting and appointments, paperwork and shopping. Then we have to allocate time to relationships, starting with our inner circle and working out to the other levels of friendship.

Surround yourself with people who respect you and treat you well.
—Claudia Black

Making time for our relationships requires considerable focus and energy. When we see how little time we actually have, it's clear that we cannot spend even a few minutes on toxic relationships. They are the relationships with family members or friends that drain us of good feeling or energy. We simply do not have the time or extra energy to devote to relationships that are unmanageable, unsatisfying and unrewarding, and we often double our problems by choosing friends with similar problems.

Doing the same things over and over with the same people and expecting a different response is a clear form of insanity.
—Anonymous

As our lives change, and we change, we can add or subtract from our families of choice as circumstances dictate. Sometimes people move away, they lose interest in us or we lose interest in them. Sometimes people die. Sometimes interests change, and what we have in common with others changes. The family of choice relationship chart helps us to take stock, evaluate and clean house.

Some say that this is a cold and calculating way to look at relationships. My belief is that the relationships I want to invest in are so important to me that I need to save my energy for them. It's not important to be popular. It is important to experience intimacy and fulfillment in chosen relationships.

We need to seek out people with whom we can be honest and expect honesty in return. They need to be easy to be around. They need to understand that when we are sometimes inconsistent, negligent and busy that we still care. We need to give them that same understanding. We can be quiet with a true friend. It is enough to be together. Sometimes there will be hysterical laughter. With true friends, giving and taking comes naturally and without pressure.

Finding that One Special Person

Another major component of our social power is finding someone we want to share our lives with in a special way as partners. The following quote, attributed to the late Ann Landers, captures the kind of love involved in sharing one's life with another:

> *Love is a friendship that has caught fire. It is quiet understanding, mutual confidence, sharing and forgiving. It is loyalty through the good times and bad. It settles for less than perfection and makes allowances for weaknesses. Love is content with the present, it hopes for the future and it doesn't brood over the past. It's the day-in, day-out chronicles of irritations, problems, compromises,*

small disappointments, big victories and common goals. If you have love in your life, it can make up for a great many things you lack. If you don't have it, no matter what else there is, it is not enough.

Social power releases all the energy we need to connect with another person. Your life with your partner is part of your core connection. I describe this connection as a "coupleship." It means a passionate, spiritual, emotional and sexual commitment between two people that nurtures both. Neena and George O'Neill, authors of *Shifting Gears*, describe the dynamic energy exchange—and amplification—at work in a coupleship:

Synergy occurs when two organisms or people are brought together or combined in such a way that the end result is enhanced. The combination of the two produces a quality or effect that is more intense than what either of the two contributing parts originally had or could attain independently. Thus, in synergy, one and one make three, not just two.

Two people in love add up to three. Each person—together with the energy they generate to form that third component, quality or effect—creates the coupleship. Each person maintains his or her uniqueness as an individual, but together, they also maintain the coupleship.

Trust, Sharing and Intimacy

It is not that we have not been loved enough, it is that we have not learned how to love.

—Sam Hardy

All happy, intimate relationships contain the following elements: trust, respect, encouragement, forgiveness, sharing of feelings, fun, sex and a spiritual quest. It is only in romance novels that great relationships happen spontaneously. A great relationship really happens as two people come to know and trust each other fully and make the choices that allow intimacy to flourish.

The cornerstone of intimacy is shared feelings, and one of the most important elements in sharing is trust. Trust builds slowly in a relationship and depends on honesty. It's like storing up an energy reserve on which the couple will draw when they face the challenges that come in every relationship. The more they trust, the more intimacy they will have.

If you listen to your conscience, it will serve you as no other friend you'll ever know. To cheat oneself out of love is the most terrible deception; it is an eternal loss for which there is no reparation, either in time or in eternity.

—Søren Kierkegaard

When trust is violated, it takes a long time to rebuild. Trust can only be rebuilt with continued actions that demonstrate that trust has been reestablished. It's not enough just to plug a line back into the socket to renew the flow of energy between two partners. Instead, the whole energy infrastructure of the relationship has to be rebuilt, from power plant to wall outlet, and tested repeatedly for reliability.

Spiritual Divorce

Unfortunately, people can make poor choices in partners when they simply want to be with someone. They may want to stop being single, to leave a marriage they are in or to just find something new and different. It is about moving on rather than dealing with where they are and what they are feeling.

People stay in unhappy relationships for different reasons. It may be because it's easier than leaving, or they don't want to disappoint anyone. They may want the financial or emotional security, or the intellectual companionship. It's more about fulfilling a need than it is about mutual love and respect.

For those in such relationships, the prognosis is bleak. A "spiritual divorce" may come long before a legal divorce. A spiritual divorce occurs when the spirit in a relationship dies. The couple may end up living together, keeping up the facade of harmony and a pretense of togetherness. They may even think the relationship is okay. But they share less, hold on to past resentments and are too busy for each other. The joyful spirit of coupleship is absent.

Such relationships take a lot out of each of the partners. They are vulnerable to affairs, and their health may suffer. Both partners feel empty, and people around them sense that something is wrong. Their quality of life has been compromised. These couples need to be honest with each other. They need to end the relationship—or commit to it and do the work to improve it so they can get on with their lives. Divorced people can be architects of a new relationship, not victims of an old relationship.

Affairs

Affairs are most likely to occur when a relationship is already damaged and unfulfilling. Whether its known to both partners, a spiritual divorce has already taken place. One or both partners seek to find intimacy with a new partner. When the affair ends, the partner will likely seek another affair unless the marriage is healed. Author Nathaniel Branden points out that after the superficial erotic novelty of an affair has faded, flattered and fled, with all the life stories told and sexual tricks played out, the adventure will cease. Then it becomes necessary to find a new partner. The person who seeks multiple partners does not experience the power and joy of commitment. There is no sustained exchange because it's not a full connection. So the energy flares and fizzles, and the relationship goes dead.

Reenergizing a Relationship

Relationships wither and die from a lack of energy; they can also be revived with an infusion of energy that helps reconnect the partners. Here are a dozen ways that couples can bring new vitality to a tired relationship.

- Plan some *timeless time* together. Timeless time is unscheduled time to do things you both enjoy.
- Give three unexpected hugs per day.
- Find one hobby to share.
- Leave notes around the house that remind your partner that you love him or her. (My partner leaves a love note on the coffeepot when he leaves early for golf.)
- Buy flowers for your partner. (People love to get flowers.)
- Take a sunrise or sunset walk together.
- Make a phone call together to an old friend. (We like to surprise mutual friends on their birthdays, an anniversary or holiday.)
- Tell your partner one of your fears. (This is good after you have gone to bed and lit a candle in the bedroom.)
- Cuddle together at bedtime or in the morning when you awaken, and tell your partner that you feel safe with him or her. (If you can't do this one, better look at why not.)
- Sit outside for an hour after dark, look at the stars and share your day.
- Pick a movie, eat popcorn and hold hands.
- Touch your partner when they least expect it. (Often, my soul mate takes my hand at a stoplight. I love

to sneak up from behind and give him a hug when he doesn't expect it.)

The energy and power released when you attend to your social power will bring great comfort and satisfaction to your life.

Helpful Reading

Divorce Recovery Sourcebook, Dawn Bradley Berry, Lowell House, 1998.

The Friendship Crisis, Marla Paul, Rodale Publishing, 2004.

Peoplemaking, Virginia Satir, Science & Behavior, 1981, second edition 1989.

The Notebook, Nicolas Sparks, Warner Books, 1996.

Coupleship, Sharon Wegscheider-Cruse, Health Communications, 1988.

Life after Divorce, Sharon Wegscheider-Cruse, Health Communications, 1994.

Family Reconstruction, Sharon Wegscheider-Cruse, (Klontz, Rainey & Higby), Science and Behavior, 1994.

Social Power Generators: Homework

- **Evaluate** the quality of your friendships. How are your relationships with your inner circle and golden and silver friends?

  _____

  _____

  _____

  _____

- **Complete** the family of choice chart (page 108) and update it on a monthly basis. Are there people you would like to move from one category to another?

  _____

  _____

  _____

  _____

- **End** toxic relationships. Identify relationships that no longer have positive energy, and begin the steps to end these relationships:

  _____

  _____

  _____

  _____

- **Nurture** existing, fulfilling relationships. Find little ways to let someone know how much you care. Who do you want to acknowledge, and how will you do it?

  _____

  _____

  _____

  _____

If you are in a primary relationship, there are additional ways to develop social balance:

• **Evaluate** the coupleship. Do you and your partner have a sense of intimacy in most areas of your lives?

_____

_____

_____

_____

• **Decide** to commit to or change the relationship. Is this relationship where you want to be?

_____

_____

_____

_____

• **Plan** to add energy to the relationship. What can you do to improve each area of this relationship?

_____

_____

_____

_____

• **Ask.** What do you want to ask for from your partner?

_____

_____

_____

_____

Social Power Journal   Week # ____

On a scale of 1 to 10, I would rate the quality of my primary relationship (if applicable) as a _____.
Areas of improvement (if applicable) include:

_____

_____

_____

_____

_____

_____

On a scale of 1 to 10, I would rate the quality of my current family relationships as a _____.
Areas of improvement (if applicable) include:

_____

_____

_____

_____

_____

_____

On a scale of 1 to 10, I would rate the quality of my past family relationships as a _____.
Areas of improvement (if applicable) include:

_____

_____

_____

_____

_____

I am/am not satisfied with the quality of my current friendships: _____. The ones I would like to change are:

_____

_____

_____

_____

_____

I am/am not trustworthy in my relationships: _____. Success or difficulties I have with this issue include:

_____

_____

_____

_____

_____

I am/am not open and honest in my relationships: _____. Success or difficulties I have with this issue include:

_____

_____

_____

_____

_____

I am/am not able to communicate clearly: _____. Success or difficulties I have with this issue include:

_____

_____

_____

_____

_____

Social Power Journal   Week # _____

On a scale of 1 to 10, I would rate the quality of my primary relationship (if applicable) as a _____.
Areas of improvement (if applicable) include:

_____

_____

_____

_____

_____

_____

On a scale of 1 to 10, I would rate the quality of my current family relationships as a _____.
Areas of improvement (if applicable) include:

_____

_____

_____

_____

_____

_____

On a scale of 1 to 10, I would rate the quality of my past family relationships as a _____.
Areas of improvement (if applicable) include:

_____

_____

_____

_____

_____

I am/am not satisfied with the quality of my current friendships: _____. The ones I would like to change are:

_____

_____

_____

_____

_____

I am/am not trustworthy in my relationships: _____. Success or difficulties I have with this issue include:

_____

_____

_____

_____

_____

I am/am not open and honest in my relationships: _____. Success or difficulties I have with this issue include:

_____

_____

_____

_____

_____

I am/am not able to communicate clearly: _____. Success or difficulties I have with this issue include:

_____

_____

_____

_____

_____

Social Power Journal   Week # ___

On a scale of 1 to 10, I would rate the quality of my primary relationship (if applicable) as a _____.
Areas of improvement (if applicable) include:

_____

_____

_____

_____

_____

On a scale of 1 to 10, I would rate the quality of my current family relationships as a _____.
Areas of improvement (if applicable) include:

_____

_____

_____

_____

_____

On a scale of 1 to 10, I would rate the quality of my past family relationships as a _____.
Areas of improvement (if applicable) include:

_____

_____

_____

_____

_____

I am/am not satisfied with the quality of my current friendships: _____. The ones I would like to change are:

_____

_____

_____

_____

_____

I am/am not trustworthy in my relationships: _____. Success or difficulties I have with this issue include:

_____

_____

_____

_____

_____

I am/am not open and honest in my relationships: _____. Success or difficulties I have with this issue include:

_____

_____

_____

_____

_____

I am/am not able to communicate clearly: _____. Success or difficulties I have with this issue include:

_____

_____

_____

_____

_____

Social Power Journal   Week # ____

On a scale of 1 to 10, I would rate the quality of my primary relationship (if applicable) as a _____.
Areas of improvement (if applicable) include:

_____

_____

_____

_____

_____

_____

On a scale of 1 to 10, I would rate the quality of my current family relationships as a _____.
Areas of improvement (if applicable) include:

_____

_____

_____

_____

_____

_____

On a scale of 1 to 10, I would rate the quality of my past family relationships as a _____.
Areas of improvement (if applicable) include:

_____

_____

_____

_____

_____

I am/am not satisfied with the quality of my current friendships: _____. The ones I would like to change are:

_____

_____

_____

_____

_____

I am/am not trustworthy in my relationships: _____. Success or difficulties I have with this issue include:

_____

_____

_____

_____

_____

I am/am not open and honest in my relationships: _____. Success or difficulties I have with this issue include:

_____

_____

_____

_____

_____

I am/am not able to communicate clearly: _____. Success or difficulties I have with this issue include:

_____

_____

_____

_____

_____

Social Power Journal   Week # ____

On a scale of 1 to 10, I would rate the quality of my primary relationship (if applicable) as a _____.
Areas of improvement (if applicable) include:

_____

_____

_____

_____

_____

_____

On a scale of 1 to 10, I would rate the quality of my current family relationships as a _____.
Areas of improvement (if applicable) include:

_____

_____

_____

_____

_____

On a scale of 1 to 10, I would rate the quality of my past family relationships as a _____.
Areas of improvement (if applicable) include:

_____

_____

_____

_____

_____

I am/am not satisfied with the quality of my current friendships: _____. The ones I would like to change are:

_____

_____

_____

_____

_____

I am/am not trustworthy in my relationships: _____. Success or difficulties I have with this issue include:

_____

_____

_____

_____

_____

I am/am not open and honest in my relationships: _____. Success or difficulties I have with this issue include:

_____

_____

_____

_____

_____

I am/am not able to communicate clearly: _____. Success or difficulties I have with this issue include:

_____

_____

_____

_____

_____

Social Power Journal   Week # ____

On a scale of 1 to 10, I would rate the quality of my primary relationship (if applicable) as a _____.
Areas of improvement (if applicable) include:

_____

_____

_____

_____

_____

_____

On a scale of 1 to 10, I would rate the quality of my current family relationships as a _____.
Areas of improvement (if applicable) include:

_____

_____

_____

_____

_____

_____

On a scale of 1 to 10, I would rate the quality of my past family relationships as a _____.
Areas of improvement (if applicable) include:

_____

_____

_____

_____

_____

I am/am not satisfied with the quality of my current friendships: _____. The ones I would like to change are:

_____

_____

_____

_____

_____

I am/am not trustworthy in my relationships: _____. Success or difficulties I have with this issue include:

_____

_____

_____

_____

_____

I am/am not open and honest in my relationships: _____. Success or difficulties I have with this issue include:

_____

_____

_____

_____

_____

I am/am not able to communicate clearly: _____. Success or difficulties I have with this issue include:

_____

_____

_____

_____

_____

Social Power Journal　　　　　　Week # ____

On a scale of 1 to 10, I would rate the quality of my primary relationship (if applicable) as a _____.
Areas of improvement (if applicable) include:

_____

_____

_____

_____

_____

_____

On a scale of 1 to 10, I would rate the quality of my current family relationships as a _____.
Areas of improvement (if applicable) include:

_____

_____

_____

_____

_____

_____

On a scale of 1 to 10, I would rate the quality of my past family relationships as a _____.
Areas of improvement (if applicable) include:

_____

_____

_____

_____

_____

I am/am not satisfied with the quality of my current friendships: _____. The ones I would like to change are:

_____

_____

_____

_____

_____

I am/am not trustworthy in my relationships: _____. Success or difficulties I have with this issue include:

_____

_____

_____

_____

_____

I am/am not open and honest in my relationships: _____. Success or difficulties I have with this issue include:

_____

_____

_____

_____

_____

I am/am not able to communicate clearly: _____. Success or difficulties I have with this issue include:

_____

_____

_____

_____

_____

Social Power Journal   Week # ____

On a scale of 1 to 10, I would rate the quality of my primary relationship (if applicable) as a _____.
Areas of improvement (if applicable) include:

_____

_____

_____

_____

_____

_____

On a scale of 1 to 10, I would rate the quality of my current family relationships as a _____.
Areas of improvement (if applicable) include:

_____

_____

_____

_____

_____

_____

On a scale of 1 to 10, I would rate the quality of my past family relationships as a _____.
Areas of improvement (if applicable) include:

_____

_____

_____

_____

_____

I am/am not satisfied with the quality of my current friendships: _____. The ones I would like to change are:

_____

_____

_____

_____

_____

I am/am not trustworthy in my relationships: _____. Success or difficulties I have with this issue include:

_____

_____

_____

_____

_____

I am/am not open and honest in my relationships: _____. Success or difficulties I have with this issue include:

_____

_____

_____

_____

_____

I am/am not able to communicate clearly: _____. Success or difficulties I have with this issue include:

_____

_____

_____

_____

_____

6

PHYSICAL POWER

*H*e who has health has hope, and he who has hope has everything.

Arabian Proverb

Communicating with Our Bodies

Each of us is given a body at birth. It is uniquely your own—and the only one you get. It will give you great pleasure and take you through many different experiences and feelings during its lifetime. You are in charge of this body, and how well it serves you depends in large measure on the care you devote to it.

Our bodies are the foundation of health, strength, endurance, beauty, agility, sensory awareness, sexual satisfaction and much, much more. All of our other powers rely on our physical selves to house them. A well-developed and cared for body has the capacity to generate the physical power that is key to experiencing many of life's joys. We use our eyes to see the people we love, an orange sunset, a beautiful flower or a majestic mountain. We use our ears to recognize a baby's cry, enjoy music and hear someone say, "I love you." We smell an apple pie, a rose, a loved one's familiar scent on a sweater. We love the touch of a hug, the comfort of a massage, the warmth of a baby snuggled close to our chest. Taste brings us pleasure in food and drink, the quenching of thirst with clear, cold water and the good feelings that go with fun foods such as popcorn, pizza and hot dogs.

The very word "HEALTH" means "WHOLE."

—Jon Kabat-Zinn

Body Types

There are several elements that come together to generate our physical power: good health, a functional and useful body, a good self-image, and a healthy sensuality

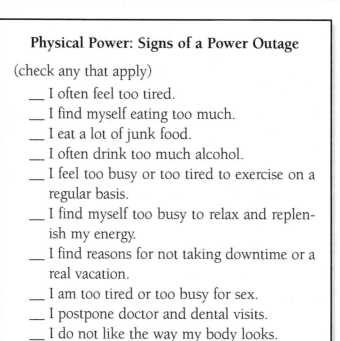

Physical Power: Signs of a Power Outage

(check any that apply)

__ I often feel too tired.

__ I find myself eating too much.

__ I eat a lot of junk food.

__ I often drink too much alcohol.

__ I feel too busy or too tired to exercise on a regular basis.

__ I find myself too busy to relax and replenish my energy.

__ I find reasons for not taking downtime or a real vacation.

__ I am too tired or too busy for sex.

__ I postpone doctor and dental visits.

__ I do not like the way my body looks.

and sexuality. The bodies we receive at birth come in all sizes, shapes and colors. Genetics determine the color of our skin, eyes and hair. How well we care for the bodies we get, however, determines how well they serve us. If we were lucky, we learned early how to nourish and exercise our bodies to bring them to their maximum potential. If we weren't so lucky, we have had to learn those lessons on our own, over time, to sustain our health.

> *The first wealth is health.*
> —*Ralph Waldo Emerson*

We can think of ourselves as healthy or unhealthy. I remember many years ago when I was diagnosed with two serious diseases on the same day. The

> *Only I can change my life. No one can do it for me.*
> —*Carol Burnett*

> *One cannot think well, love well, or sleep well, if one has not dined well.*
>
> *—Virginia Woolf*

first was breast cancer, and the second was cardiomyopathy, heart disease. I had experienced no symptoms; I was simply going to my annual physical exam. Until that day, I believed and lived as though I were perfectly healthy. In fact, I had been at a health spa the week before and had hiked a total of sixty-three miles feeling very good and very much in charge of my life.

The diagnoses were a big shock to me, and I immediately set out to face the two illnesses and get back to normal. I had a big decision to make at that time. For me, "normal" meant feeling in charge of my physical body and believing myself to be a healthy person. When the treatments for both of my illnesses were complete, I had a choice of seeing myself as an *unhealthy person* with two diseases or a *healthy person who could manage my illnesses.* I chose the latter.

> *People who exercise, whether that involves an intense workout or just a regular long walk, feel healthier, feel better about themselves and enjoy life more.*
>
> *—David Niven*

It has been quite a challenge for me to set aside time each day to do my three-mile walk, attend aerobic classes and eat the right foods. It means some other things in my life needed to change, and I had to rearrange my priorities. But the rewards of following through on my commitment to my health have been enormous.

Life Can Be Hard on a Body

Life happens to all of us. There will be accidents, illnesses, aging and events beyond our control. However, as author Joan Borysenko says, "Life is filled with changes. Whether we can cope with those changes or not will determine whether we will grow with the situation or be overcome by it, whether we will act helplessly or have hope. People who feel in control of life can withstand an enormous amount of change and thrive on it."

Energy Sources, Exercise and Looking Good

The foods we eat and the exercise we take will strongly influence how our bodies will function and how much energy will be available to enjoy our lives. Will we give our bodies foods that generate energy or drain it? Will we transform all the food into energy, or will there be excess that turns to fat and causes health problems? Good nutrition is a responsibility. It's important to spend time learning about how to provide our bodies with proper nourishment. Even the time we take to eat is a challenge. Do we make good choices or do we simply pick the easiest, most appealing items? If we make poor choices, we have to suffer the consequences of weight gain or poor health. Healthful eating, however, generates a great deal of personal power.

Experiences of wholeness are as accessible to people with chronic illness or stress-related problems as they are to anyone else.

—*Author Unknown*

Our bodies also require and respond very positively to exercise, which generates a feeling of well-being and satisfaction. There are lots of ways to get exercise, from walking, running, swimming and working out at the gym to yoga, aerobics, dancing and even gardening—whatever keeps you active. I especially love exercises that not only release positive energy but also give me a feeling of joy. I have learned that I owe my body exercise if I expect it to be a reliable energy source. That's why I commit to exercising five days a week—and every day if I want to release even more power.

When we eat well and exercise regularly, we're much more likely to become and remain healthy. Most healthy people want to look good. Looking good starts with weight control and includes good grooming, an attractive hairstyle and wearing well-made clothes that complement our shape. Looking good sends the message that we care about ourselves, because we care about our appearance. It also helps us feel better.

When I was onstage a great deal of the time, I was always aware that when I felt that I looked good, it was easier for me to walk to the podium and speak. Looking as good as I could gave me an energy boost and made me feel stronger and more confident. I think it does the same for most people.

Sensual Power Surges

Being able to enjoy our sensual nature opens a world of experience that truly empowers us. To savor the contact that our senses enable is one key to finding satisfaction in life. Touch, smell, sight, sound and taste all have the potential to bring us excitement, pleasure and fulfillment. Life surges into us through the senses in many ways: hugging someone we care about, watching a colorful sunset, hearing a concert or savoring a luscious chocolate dessert.

Some of the most sensual people I know are not in a current primary relationship. Yet they are bursting with energy, spirit and passion. They are connected with their feelings—their passion for life. After all, the root word for "passion" means *full of feeling.*

We can be passionate about many things. Our five senses feed our passion. When we actually feel our feelings, and not just talk about them, we have a passion-filled experience. We all know how it feels to experience:

- deeper breathing when we're aroused
- a faster heartbeat when we are afraid
- relaxed muscles when we laugh or are massaged
- flushed skin when we're embarrassed
- a raised voice when we're angry

When we are open to our senses and to sensual experiences, we get to live life to the fullest. Take a minute to get in touch with your senses. Close your eyes, imagine the following experiences and sense what they would be like:

- smelling a flower, a cinnamon roll, perfume, the ocean, a horse stable, a Christmas tree
- hearing music, a fountain, birds chirping, drums beating, a standing ovation, an argument
- tasting pizza, popcorn, chocolate, ice cream, a salad, a cheeseburger, good coffee
- touching/sharing a hug, silk, leather, a hot shower, a kiss, a massage, a down comforter

- seeing a crimson sunset; majestic mountains; a familiar, loved face; a warm smile; the ocean.

All of these experiences awaken part of our physical power. They are all aspects of our sensory power, and they have the potential of bringing great satisfaction and pleasure.

Sexual Power Surges

Sexuality is another very important part of fulfilling our physical potential, and it plays a lifelong role in our well-being. There is the awakening sexuality of a young person, full of exploration and part of defining who we become. There is the passion we spend when we make love with someone we love. There is the power of the body being able to give birth. There is comfort in holding hands, snuggling, hugging and touching. Sexuality has a role in every stage of life.

Emotional Intercourse

In order to feel safe sharing our passion and feelings with another, we also need to develop safety ("You will honor my feelings") and trust ("You will not hurt me"). When safety, trust and sharing all come together, there is intimacy. I call this intimacy "emotional intercourse." The fulfillment of sex is directly related to the quality of intimacy that precedes physical contact.

Physical Intercourse

Another step in embracing our physical power is exploring physical contact (affection) and intercourse. Healthy people do not share core feelings (emotional intercourse) with just anyone. As said before, they want safety and trust. Healthy people do not share their bodies with just anyone either. They also want safety and trust, as well as honesty and caring.

When people have physical sex without emotion and passion, they often say they feel empty and lonely, although they have a great deal of sexual activity. The hunger they are looking to fill isn't found in more sex—it's intimacy they are craving. Intimacy is shared emotion and feelings. Without it, sex can become totally mechanical and nonfulfilling.

Mechanical Sex

Mechanical sex occurs when someone is aroused *only* by external, artificial stimulation, and there is an absence of feelings and emotion. The most frequently used artificial stimulations are chronic masturbation, pornography, affairs, and violence and danger—that is, living on the edge and needing excess excitement in one's life.

Developing a healthy sex life is a challenge in today's society. One of the most common sexual problems that couples report to marriage counselors is lack of desire. They report that they are too busy, too tired or just not interested. After a while, people develop a comfortable arrangement in which they don't even talk about sex anymore. It's a loss for both partners.

Sexual Basics and Barriers

Relationships and intimacy are choices. When our sensory system is awake, and we are able to feel, we have a tool that is called "sensate focus." That means that at any time, we have the power to focus on any part of our body and bring attention to it. We can focus on sight, sound, smell, taste and touch. If we are feeling safe and trusting and good about the person we are with, we also have the ability to focus on our genitals and become physically aroused.

It is no one's job to make us feel aroused. It is each person's job to arouse himself or herself using sensate focus. We can do this because of our personally developed passion. When we have allowed our true feelings to surface, we will be "full of feeling" (passionate). We will then be able to experience emotional intimacy with our partner. It will make the move to physical intimacy easy and fulfilling. This creates the high called an orgasm. We will have a full body orgasm that includes emotion and feeling, not just a genital orgasm that involves only bodies. A full orgasm is felt both in the heart *and* in the genitals. It is very pleasurable and satisfying.

Love is shown by deeds, not by words.

—Author Unknown

Unfortunately, not everyone has this kind of satisfying sex. The primary barriers to good sex are:

1. Medicated feelings (chemical)
   • nicotine
   • excess alcohol
   • drugs and medication
2. Old feelings
   • childhood sexual abuse
   • date rape
   • betrayal by an affair
3. Medicated feelings (behavioral)
   • workaholism
   • excess exercise
   • busyness, excess fatigue

Ignoring our physical power can bring about great stress. Developing our physical power can bring great satisfaction, a sense of well-being and joy.

Helpful Reading

High Level Wellness, Donald B. Ardell, Rodale Press, 1977.

Minding The Body, Mending The Mind, Joan Borysenko, Bantam, 1987.

Anatomy of an Illness, Norman Cousins, Norton, 1979.

Fitness Walking, Therese Ikonian, Human Kinetics Publishing, Inc., 1995.

Peace, Love & Healing, Bernie Siegel, Harper & Row, 1990.

Aging Well, George Valliant, Little Brown & Co., 2004.

Eating Well for Optimum Health, Andrew Weil, M.D., Quill Publishing, 2001.

Helpful Resources

Two wonderful resources for exploring one's personal powers are the Miraval Life in Balance Spa in Tuscon, Arizona (*www.miravallifeinbalance.com*), and the Red Mountain Spa in St. George, Utah (*www.redmountain spa.com*). These spas specialize in helping people find balance in their lives. They provide activities for mind, body and spirit. I have personally spent a great deal of time at both spas, and they have helped me balance my life.

Physical Power Generators: Homework

- **Commit** to a plan of good nutrition. What changes can you make in your daily eating that would be good for you?

  _____

  _____

  _____

  _____

  _____

- **Start** moving and exercising on a regular basis immediately. What do you have to change to guarantee that you exercise either one-half hour or one full hour each day?

  _____

  _____

  _____

  _____

  _____

- **Enjoy** sensuality. Take time to listen to a special song, purchase a particular flower, wear clothes that make you feel good. What other way can you wake up your sensuality?

  _____

  _____

  _____

  _____

  _____

- **Explore** sexuality. Do you like being a woman or a man? Are you in a relationship or are you single? Are you comfortable with your sexual orientation? Evaluate your own situation, then read books, talk with your partner or friends, join groups and move in the direction of what you want and need. What questions do you ask yourself about your sexuality?

_____

_____

_____

_____

_____

_____

What action or actions do you want to take?

_____

_____

_____

_____

_____

Physical Power Journal   Week # ____

What is my plan for regular exercise, and how well am I doing?

_____

_____

_____

_____

_____

What is my plan for good nutrition and eating well, and how am I doing ?

_____

_____

_____

_____

_____

What are my sleeping patterns and do I get enough rest? If not, what am I going to do about it?

_____

_____

_____

_____

_____

How is my health in general? Am I making sure I get medical and dental checkups on a regular basis? If not, what am I going to do about it?

_____

_____

_____

_____

Am I satisfied with my body image? If not, what are my plans for changing it, and what am I doing right now to meet those goals?

_____

_____

_____

_____

_____

_____

_____

What am I doing to awaken my sensuality?

_____

_____

_____

_____

_____

_____

What am I doing to enhance my sexuality?

_____

_____

_____

_____

_____

_____

Physical Power Journal   Week # ___

What is my plan for regular exercise, and how well am I doing?

_____

_____

_____

_____

_____

What is my plan for good nutrition and eating well, and how am I doing ?

_____

_____

_____

_____

_____

What are my sleeping patterns and do I get enough rest? If not, what am I going to do about it?

_____

_____

_____

_____

_____

How is my health in general? Am I making sure I get medical and dental checkups on a regular basis? If not, what am I going to do about it?

_____

_____

_____

_____

Am I satisfied with my body image? If not, what are my plans for changing it, and what am I doing right now to meet those goals?

_____

_____

_____

_____

_____

_____

_____

What am I doing to awaken my sensuality?

_____

_____

_____

_____

_____

_____

What am I doing to enhance my sexuality?

_____

_____

_____

_____

_____

_____

Physical Power Journal   Week # ____

What is my plan for regular exercise, and how well am I doing?

_____

_____

_____

_____

_____

What is my plan for good nutrition and eating well, and how am I doing ?

_____

_____

_____

_____

_____

What are my sleeping patterns and do I get enough rest? If not, what am I going to do about it?

_____

_____

_____

_____

_____

How is my health in general? Am I making sure I get medical and dental checkups on a regular basis? If not, what am I going to do about it?

_____

_____

_____

_____

Am I satisfied with my body image? If not, what are my plans for changing it, and what am I doing right now to meet those goals?

_____

_____

_____

_____

_____

_____

_____

What am I doing to awaken my sensuality?

_____

_____

_____

_____

_____

What am I doing to enhance my sexuality?

_____

_____

_____

_____

_____

_____

Physical Power Journal   Week # ____

What is my plan for regular exercise, and how well am I doing?

_____

_____

_____

_____

_____

What is my plan for good nutrition and eating well, and how am I doing ?

_____

_____

_____

_____

_____

What are my sleeping patterns and do I get enough rest? If not, what am I going to do about it?

_____

_____

_____

_____

_____

How is my health in general? Am I making sure I get medical and dental checkups on a regular basis? If not, what am I going to do about it?

_____

_____

_____

_____

Am I satisfied with my body image? If not, what are my plans for changing it, and what am I doing right now to meet those goals?

_____

_____

_____

_____

_____

_____

_____

What am I doing to awaken my sensuality?

_____

_____

_____

_____

_____

_____

What am I doing to enhance my sexuality?

_____

_____

_____

_____

_____

_____

Physical Power Journal   Week # ____

What is my plan for regular exercise, and how well am I doing?

_____

_____

_____

_____

_____

What is my plan for good nutrition and eating well, and how am I doing ?

_____

_____

_____

_____

_____

What are my sleeping patterns and do I get enough rest? If not, what am I going to do about it?

_____

_____

_____

_____

_____

How is my health in general? Am I making sure I get medical and dental checkups on a regular basis? If not, what am I going to do about it?

_____

_____

_____

_____

Am I satisfied with my body image? If not, what are my plans for changing it, and what am I doing right now to meet those goals?

_____

_____

_____

_____

_____

_____

_____

What am I doing to awaken my sensuality?

_____

_____

_____

_____

_____

_____

What am I doing to enhance my sexuality?

_____

_____

_____

_____

_____

_____

Physical Power Journal   Week # ____

What is my plan for regular exercise, and how well am I doing?

_____

_____

_____

_____

_____

What is my plan for good nutrition and eating well, and how am I doing ?

_____

_____

_____

_____

_____

What are my sleeping patterns and do I get enough rest? If not, what am I going to do about it?

_____

_____

_____

_____

_____

How is my health in general? Am I making sure I get medical and dental checkups on a regular basis? If not, what am I going to do about it?

_____

_____

_____

_____

Am I satisfied with my body image? If not, what are my plans for changing it, and what am I doing right now to meet those goals?

_____

_____

_____

_____

_____

_____

_____

What am I doing to awaken my sensuality?

_____

_____

_____

_____

_____

_____

What am I doing to enhance my sexuality?

_____

_____

_____

_____

_____

_____

Physical Power Journal   Week # ____

What is my plan for regular exercise, and how well am I doing?

_____

_____

_____

_____

_____

What is my plan for good nutrition and eating well, and how am I doing ?

_____

_____

_____

_____

_____

What are my sleeping patterns and do I get enough rest? If not, what am I going to do about it?

_____

_____

_____

_____

_____

How is my health in general? Am I making sure I get medical and dental checkups on a regular basis? If not, what am I going to do about it?

_____

_____

_____

_____

Am I satisfied with my body image? If not, what are my plans for changing it, and what am I doing right now to meet those goals?

_____

_____

_____

_____

_____

_____

What am I doing to awaken my sensuality?

_____

_____

_____

_____

_____

What am I doing to enhance my sexuality?

_____

_____

_____

_____

_____

7

MENTAL POWER

*T*he energy of the mind is the essence of life.

Aristotle

Brainpower

The brain is an incredible command center for our mental power. It receives and dispenses information, accumulates knowledge and makes our life rich. Our mental power can be counted on to make much of our life automatic by storing what we have learned and then making that information available to us at all times without our having to think about it.

Wisdom is the instinctive sense of how to apply the information you have.

—Harold Kushner

Mental Mastery Never Ceases

Once we have learned how to do it, most of us can automatically eat, eliminate, walk, talk, eat, sing, whistle, cough, ride a bike, drive a car, make love and do dozens of other activities as well, with minimum effort and maximum mastery.

Follow your dreams and pursue them with courage for it is the pursuit of those dreams that makes life really worth living.

—Linda DuPuy Moore

We can also acquire and improve skills at any time by learning more and by developing more of our brainpower. We can add virtually any skill we want to our repertoire, from speaking other languages, using computers or engineering a bridge to piloting an aircraft, facilitating a group, trying a case in court or performing surgery. The list is endless and exciting because all the choices are ours.

Our mental power has three metaphorical components: the *historian,* the *dreamer* and the *realist.* Each

Mental Power: Signs of a Power Outage

(check any that apply)

___ I have few or no hobbies that I enjoy.

___ I read mostly work-related books and journals.

___ It's been a long time since I developed a new skill.

___ I tend to avoid nonproductive efforts (fantasies and dreams).

___ I work more than a forty-hour week.

___ I find most of my fulfillment through work.

___ I always seem to be short of money.

___ I rarely have money saved for big ticket items (cars, vacations, housing, etc.).

___ I pay more than I would like to because I am always paying interest.

___ I often pay top dollar and make poor choices.

___ I am afraid to follow my passions and my dreams.

___ I have trouble looking at all aspects of a decision if it doesn't fit my preconceived ideas or plans.

___ It's hard for me to be open to new ideas and ways of doing things.

___ I have difficulty asking for help.

component has a specific job to do and a special contribution to make to our well-being.

The Historian

Home is the heart of life. Home is where we feel at ease, where we belong, where we can create surroundings that reflect our tastes and pleasures. Making a home is a form of creativity open to everyone.

—Terence Conran

This part of our brain captures, shapes and holds all of our memory. It's the part that enables us to walk, talk and eat without thinking about it. It records what we learn and allows us to retrieve that knowledge almost without effort. Physical skills and intellectual learning are ours to keep. The historian also stores emotional memories. It's easy to remember the good times we have had—the joys of birthdays, the happiness of graduations, the fun of vacations and the thrill of falling in love. The historian stores all our special memories. It also stores painful memories, losses we have had, plans that didn't work out and harm that may have come our way. Memory is a wonderful function. We can celebrate the good memories, and we have options for healing the painful ones.

Imagination is more important than knowledge.

—Albert Einstein

It is important to keep our memory banks clean and current. It's a wonderful resource and a storehouse of useful information and pleasurable moments. However, we must remember that although we can visit our memory banks, we don't want to live there. Sometimes people get stuck in the past, and it inhibits growth in the other two areas of mental life.

The historian can grow by taking a class, learning to play the piano or keyboard, going to cooking school, taking golf lessons or reading a good book. He or she may keep scrapbooks, do family genealogy, take photographs, or put together family or class reunions. Historians have a special link to the past and enjoy spending time recreating it.

If there has been pain in the past, the historian may profit from doing some family therapy. There is a wonderful book and workshop available that will help historians revisit old memories of childhood, divorce, abuse and loss. Then they can heal and move on. The book and workshop are both called *Family Reconstruction* and are available from Onsite Workshops at *www.onsite workshops.com.*

The Dreamer

Dreaming, imagining, fantasizing and inventing are necessary to be a whole person. If we didn't have dreamers, we wouldn't have electricity, telephones, cell phones or computers. We wouldn't have medical breakthroughs or an entertainment industry. It is the combination of the soul, the heart and mental power of imagination that gives us most inventions and improvements in our lives.

> **Nothing happens unless it is first a dream.**
> —*Carl Sandburg*

Dreamers can grow by making plans, taking trips, trying new ventures. They can write books, redecorate their homes, and go to movies and plays. Dreamers can walk in the woods, lie on the beach, watch birds or work in the garden and see what comes to them in those moments of reflection. Dreamers can meditate and let their minds wander. Their mental power is bound to send them messages and many of those messages may be inspired.

The Realist

The realist lives in the present. The realist knows that we must have food, shelter, clothing, education and mobility. In order to have those things we must have enough money to buy them. The realist also knows that to pursue dreams and interests takes money and time. It is clear that in order to have the time to do things, we need to be earning money the rest of the time. The realist knows that the accumulation of wealth and resulting financial security certainly give us the time and freedom to have more choices in life. The realists in us hold jobs, save money, and learn about investing and generating passive income. Emotions are often tied up with these money issues. Too much money or too little money can be a great source of personal conflict and pain. It's important to have an understanding of our financial selves and how we choose to live.

Do what you love and the money will follow.
—*Marsha Sinetar*

Realists can grow by making lists, planning investments and learning about opportunities for creating financial security. They can go to work each day and fulfill responsibilities. They make doctor and dentist appointments. They pay taxes and do the grocery shopping. They get the car serviced and they pay bills. Life events occur so rapidly that if we are preoccupied with the past, like the historian, or imagining the future, like the dreamer we may miss the opportunities—and responsibilities—of the present. The realist takes care of all that.

Genius is that energy which collects, combines, amplifies and animates.
—*Samuel Johnson*

Integration of the Historian, Dreamer and Realist

When you put all the components of mental power together, it's clear that this power is a huge and important part of us. It deserves to be continually developed. The mind also deserves to rest a good seven to eight hours each day. Mental power needs both relaxation and sleep because, when it is active, it uses a great deal of energy. Much of that energy is exacting. When someone is flying an airplane, taking care of children, performing surgery, driving a car or making important decisions, you want that person's mental powers sharp and alert—not sleep deprived.

Do what intrigues you, explore what interests you. Think mystery, not mastery.

—*Julie Cameron*

If we neglect any part of our mental power, we run the risk of being left behind in an ever-changing world. For example, if we become limited historians, we risk becoming boring and listless and developing only the memory part of our mental power. We may then be caught in the past, unable to experience the great possibilities this vast world offers us. If we only develop the dreamer-oriented ideas and technical parts of our mental power, we may become nerdy and antisocial. If we let the realist part of our brain dominate, we can become stuffy and not much fun to be around. We need to be using all components of our mental power all the time.

Painting is just another way of keeping a diary.

—*Pablo Picasso*

Helpful Reading

Becoming a Writer, Dorothea Brande, Jeremy P. Tarcher,
1981.

Money Drunk, Money Sober, Mark Bryan and Julie
Cameron, Ballantine Books, 1992.

Your Heart's Desire, Sonie Choquette, Random House,
1997.

If Not Now, When, Stephanie Marston, Warner Books,
2001.

Mental Power Generators: Homework

For the Historian in You:

• **Read** a book and learn something new. What are you working on this week?

_____

_____

_____

_____

_____

• **Enroll** in a class. Study a new language, cooking, travel, scrapbooking, parenting or dance, among others. Do something really fun and different. What do you want to do, what's your plan for doing it, and when will you start?

_____

_____

_____

_____

_____

• **Visit** a friend or relative and share photos and memories. Or attend a class or family reunion. What would you like to do, what's your plan for doing it, and when will you do it?

_____

_____

_____

_____

_____

- **Release** a painful memory. If there is a memory that no longer serves you, let it go. What memory do you want to let go?

  _____

  _____

  _____

  _____

  _____

For the Dreamer in You:
- **Explore** the possibility of making a dream come true. What is your dream?

  _____

  _____

  _____

  _____

  _____

- **Plan** at least one trip (big or small) per year. What trip do you want to plan right now?

  _____

  _____

  _____

  _____

  _____

- **Choose** a movie that awakens some passion in you, and plan to see it. What movie will you choose?

  _____

  _____

  _____

For the Realist in You:

- **Pay** bills and organize your financial life. What projects do you need to tackle this week?

_____

_____

_____

_____

_____

- **Invest** some money (a large or small amount). For example buy one share of stock or several shares, or invest in a mutual fund. The important thing is to start now. What are your investment plans this week, and how are you going to accomplish them?

_____

_____

_____

_____

- **Practice** self-care (for example, seeing your doctor or dentist, making car repairs, etc.). What appointments will you make and/or keep this week?

_____

_____

_____

_____

- **Start** and finish a project. What project do you want to do start, and what step or steps will you take **this week** toward accomplishing it?

  _____

  _____

  _____

  _____

  _____

- **Stay** informed, connected and involved (locally, nationally and worldwide). Give your attention to some informative news shows, newspapers and periodicals. How will you do that this week?

  _____

  _____

  _____

  _____

  _____

Mental Power Journal   Week # ____

I am involved in new learning experiences. Some of those experiences are:

_____

_____

_____

_____

_____

I am open to new ideas and change. One thing that I want to explore and learn more about is:

_____

_____

_____

_____

_____

Have I healed my past memories, and am I ready to move on? Some of those memories include:

_____

_____

_____

_____

_____

How did/can I move on?

_____

_____

_____

_____

_____

I am imaginative in finding alternatives to issues that have bothered me in the past. One of example of this is:

_____

_____

_____

_____

_____

I have at least two dreams I would like to actualize. They are:

_____

_____

_____

_____

_____

I am taking steps to become more organized. To achieve that goal, this week I plan to:

_____

_____

_____

_____

_____

My next plan is:

_____

_____

_____

_____

_____

I have plans to improve my financial situation. These plans include:

_____

_____

_____

_____

_____

My first step in accomplishing these plans is to:

_____

_____

_____

_____

_____

My next step is:

_____

_____

_____

_____

_____

Enjoying satisfying hobbies:

_____

_____

_____

_____

_____

Mental Power Journal   Week # ____

I am involved in new learning experiences. Some of those experiences are:

_____

_____

_____

_____

I am open to new ideas and change. One thing that I want to explore and learn more about is:

_____

_____

_____

_____

Have I healed my past memories, and am I ready to move on? Some of those memories include:

_____

_____

_____

_____

How did/can I move on?

_____

_____

_____

_____

I am imaginative in finding alternatives to issues that have bothered me in the past. One of example of this is:

_____

_____

_____

_____

_____

I have at least two dreams I would like to actualize. They are:

_____

_____

_____

_____

_____

I am taking steps to become more organized. To achieve that goal, this week I plan to:

_____

_____

_____

_____

_____

My next plan is:

_____

_____

_____

_____

_____

I have plans to improve my financial situation. These plans include:

_____

_____

_____

_____

_____

My first step in accomplishing these plans is to:

_____

_____

_____

_____

_____

My next step is:

_____

_____

_____

_____

_____

Enjoying satisfying hobbies:

_____

_____

_____

_____

_____

Mental Power Journal   Week # ____

I am involved in new learning experiences. Some of those experiences are:

_____

_____

_____

_____

_____

I am open to new ideas and change. One thing that I want to explore and learn more about is:

_____

_____

_____

_____

Have I healed my past memories, and am I ready to move on? Some of those memories include:

_____

_____

_____

_____

How did/can I move on?

_____

_____

_____

_____

I am imaginative in finding alternatives to issues that have bothered me in the past. One of example of this is:

_____

_____

_____

_____

_____

I have at least two dreams I would like to actualize. They are:

_____

_____

_____

_____

_____

I am taking steps to become more organized. To achieve that goal, this week I plan to:

_____

_____

_____

_____

_____

My next plan is:

_____

_____

_____

_____

_____

I have plans to improve my financial situation. These plans include:

_____

_____

_____

_____

_____

My first step in accomplishing these plans is to:

_____

_____

_____

_____

My next step is:

_____

_____

_____

_____

Enjoying satisfying hobbies:

_____

_____

_____

_____

Mental Power Journal   Week # ____

I am involved in new learning experiences. Some of those experiences are:

_____

_____

_____

_____

_____

I am open to new ideas and change. One thing that I want to explore and learn more about is:

_____

_____

_____

_____

_____

Have I healed my past memories, and am I ready to move on? Some of those memories include:

_____

_____

_____

_____

_____

How did/can I move on?

_____

_____

_____

_____

I am imaginative in finding alternatives to issues that have bothered me in the past. One of example of this is:

_____

_____

_____

_____

_____

I have at least two dreams I would like to actualize. They are:

_____

_____

_____

_____

_____

I am taking steps to become more organized. To achieve that goal, this week I plan to:

_____

_____

_____

_____

_____

My next plan is:

_____

_____

_____

_____

I have plans to improve my financial situation. These plans include:

_____

_____

_____

_____

_____

My first step in accomplishing these plans is to:

_____

_____

_____

_____

My next step is:

_____

_____

_____

_____

Enjoying satisfying hobbies:

_____

_____

_____

_____

Mental Power Journal   Week # ____

I am involved in new learning experiences. Some of those experiences are:

_____

_____

_____

_____

_____

I am open to new ideas and change. One thing that I want to explore and learn more about is:

_____

_____

_____

_____

_____

Have I healed my past memories, and am I ready to move on? Some of those memories include:

_____

_____

_____

_____

_____

How did/can I move on?

_____

_____

_____

_____

_____

I am imaginative in finding alternatives to issues that have bothered me in the past. One of example of this is:

_____

_____

_____

_____

_____

I have at least two dreams I would like to actualize. They are:

_____

_____

_____

_____

_____

I am taking steps to become more organized. To achieve that goal, this week I plan to:

_____

_____

_____

_____

_____

My next plan is:

_____

_____

_____

_____

_____

I have plans to improve my financial situation. These plans include:

_____

_____

_____

_____

_____

My first step in accomplishing these plans is to:

_____

_____

_____

_____

My next step is:

_____

_____

_____

_____

Enjoying satisfying hobbies:

_____

_____

_____

_____

Mental Power Journal   Week # ____

I am involved in new learning experiences. Some of those experiences are:

_____

_____

_____

_____

_____

I am open to new ideas and change. One thing that I want to explore and learn more about is:

_____

_____

_____

_____

_____

Have I healed my past memories, and am I ready to move on? Some of those memories include:

_____

_____

_____

_____

_____

How did/can I move on?

_____

_____

_____

_____

_____

I am imaginative in finding alternatives to issues that have bothered me in the past. One of example of this is:

_____

_____

_____

_____

_____

I have at least two dreams I would like to actualize. They are:

_____

_____

_____

_____

_____

I am taking steps to become more organized. To achieve that goal, this week I plan to:

_____

_____

_____

_____

_____

My next plan is:

_____

_____

_____

_____

_____

I have plans to improve my financial situation. These plans include:

_____

_____

_____

_____

_____

My first step in accomplishing these plans is to:

_____

_____

_____

_____

My next step is:

_____

_____

_____

_____

Enjoying satisfying hobbies:

_____

_____

_____

_____

Mental Power Journal   Week # ____

I am involved in new learning experiences. Some of those experiences are:

_____

_____

_____

_____

_____

I am open to new ideas and change. One thing that I want to explore and learn more about is:

_____

_____

_____

_____

_____

Have I healed my past memories, and am I ready to move on? Some of those memories include:

_____

_____

_____

_____

_____

How did/can I move on?

_____

_____

_____

_____

_____

I am imaginative in finding alternatives to issues that have bothered me in the past. One of example of this is:

_____

_____

_____

_____

_____

I have at least two dreams I would like to actualize. They are:

_____

_____

_____

_____

I am taking steps to become more organized. To achieve that goal, this week I plan to:

_____

_____

_____

_____

My next plan is:

_____

_____

_____

_____

I have plans to improve my financial situation. These plans include:

_____

_____

_____

_____

_____

My first step in accomplishing these plans is to:

_____

_____

_____

_____

_____

My next step is:

_____

_____

_____

_____

_____

Enjoying satisfying hobbies:

_____

_____

_____

_____

_____

Mental Power Journal   Week # ____

I am involved in new learning experiences. Some of those experiences are:

_____

_____

_____

_____

_____

I am open to new ideas and change. One thing that I want to explore and learn more about is:

_____

_____

_____

_____

Have I healed my past memories, and am I ready to move on? Some of those memories include:

_____

_____

_____

_____

How did/can I move on?

_____

_____

_____

_____

I am imaginative in finding alternatives to issues that have bothered me in the past. One of example of this is:

_____

_____

_____

_____

_____

I have at least two dreams I would like to actualize. They are:

_____

_____

_____

_____

_____

I am taking steps to become more organized. To achieve that goal, this week I plan to:

_____

_____

_____

_____

_____

My next plan is:

_____

_____

_____

_____

_____

I have plans to improve my financial situation. These plans include:

_____

_____

_____

_____

_____

My first step in accomplishing these plans is to:

_____

_____

_____

_____

_____

My next step is:

_____

_____

_____

_____

_____

Enjoying satisfying hobbies:

_____

_____

_____

_____

AFTERWORD

Spirit Awakened

*I*t may seem easier and less risky to cling to familiar patterns and old habits and interests. But without change there is actually a greater risk that you will miss the chance to become the person you have the power to be. There are always possibilities for new life, new choices and an exciting spirit just under the surface.

As each of us harnesses our powers and reenergizes our ability to experience life, we take our places with other spirit people who have reawakened their spirits. Each awakened spirit is like a distinct, unique note with a clear, beautiful sound. Together these notes create compelling music, sung by a chorus that inspires all who can hear.

Spirit people radiate hope, warmth, opportunity and love to others. They have the power to fill the emptiness, give direction to aimlessness and dissolve the selfishness that separates people. They replace the spiritual void with a life of meaning and fulfillment.

Each of us can be a spirit person if we only awaken and exercise the power we were born with.

Choicemaking

Every day I have before me many choices.
It is not easy to choose,
for often the choice means
letting go
of the past,
of the present.

I know what the past was.
I know what the present is.
But the choice propels me into the future.
I'm not sure I'll make the right choices.

It's not easy to "let go."
It's not easy to fly into the future.
It's like the space between trapezes.
It is not knowing whether you're going to be
    caught.
It is not knowing whether you're going to fall.

It's not easy to live in trust.
That space between trapezes requires faith.
I must admit that my faith is often shaky.
I pray and hope that I'll make good decisions,
That I'll be caught and will not fall.

Every day I have before me many choices.

—Sharon Wegscheider-Cruse

Other books by Sharon Wegscheider-Cruse

Learning to Love Yourself
Choicemaking
Life After Divorce
Coupleship
GirlTalk
Dancing with Destiny
Understanding Co-Dependency
Another Chance: Hope and Health for the Alcoholic Family
Grandparenting

For more information about books, workshops and coaching, contact *www.sharonwcruse.com.*

NOTES

NOTES

NOTES

More from our author